Wicked

WASHTENAW
COUNTY

STRANGE TALES OF THE
GRISLY AND UNEXPLAINED

JAMES THOMAS MANN

Charleston   London

THE
History
PRESS

Published by The History Press
Charleston, SC 29403
www.historypress.net

Some cover images from the collection of Laura Bien.

First published 2010

Manufactured in the United States

ISBN 978.1.59629.912.2

Library of Congress Cataloging-in-Publication Data
Mann, James Thomas.
Wicked Washtenaw county : strange tales of the grisly and unexplained / James Thomas
Mann.
p. cm.
Includes bibliographical references.
ISBN 978-1-59629-912-2
1. Washtenaw County (Mich.)--History--Anecdotes. 2. Washtenaw County (Mich.)-
-History, Local--Anecdotes. 3. Washtenaw County (Mich.)--Social life and customs-
-Anecdotes. 4. Washtenaw County (Mich.)--Biography--Anecdotes. 5. Violence--
Michigan--Washtenaw County--History--Anecdotes. 6. Death--Michigan--Washtenaw
County--History--Anecdotes. 7. Curiosities and wonders--Michigan--Washtenaw County--
History--Anecdotes. I. Title.
F572.W3M36 2010
977.4'35--dc22
2010020425

Contents

Foreword

Two sweet ladies waved at me from across the Ypsilanti Farmers' Market in the Freighthouse one Saturday morning in the early 1980s and said they had somebody they wanted me to meet. The subject of their fascination stood nearby, clutching an overstuffed manila envelope and looking scared to death. "He has some stories you might like to run in the *Depot Town Rag*," they proffered, and he timidly held out a bundle of about ten pounds of paper.

Close inspection proved that his collection was tales of terrible deaths suffered at the railroad crossing in Ypsilanti's Depot Town. Buoyed by the popularity of Michael Lesy's 1973 book, *Wisconsin Death Trip*, James Thomas Mann contended that such tragedies were common to every community, and he suggested that interest in Ypsilanti's bad news might prove just as popular with our loyal readership. We ran the first series our little neighborhood *Rag* had ever seen, and it continued for many months with great response from our readers.

Lesy's book was based on a collection of late nineteenth-century photos from Jackson County, Wisconsin, made by Charles VanScheick, mostly from stories of crime, disease and mental illness in Black River Falls. In 1975, Conrad Susa composed an opera on the theme titled *Black River*. In 1994, the band Static-X used the same title for its thrash metal album. In 2000, it was made into a black-and-white documentary movie. Australian author Rod

Jones cites *Wisconsin Death Trip* as an inspiration for his novel *Billy Sunday*, which was described as "The Great American Novel" by the *Boston Globe*.

James's series in the *Rag* had a narrower focus. It was about people who were run over by the steam engines passing from Detroit to Chicago—more direct and with more impact than those subtle tales from the other side of Lake Michigan.

James Mann's current historical interests seem to be following the same path but without his having to leave Washtenaw County. Like *Wisconsin Death Trip*'s theme, Mann's collection of bad news is terribly local and terribly terrible. Bad stuff happens to good people; it's a constant theme. It sells newspapers, too. Mann easily fits the theme established by the film's director, James Marsh: "I wanted to convey in the film the real pathos contained in a four-line newspaper report that simultaneously records and dismisses the end of someone's life."

Just as in Mann's "Depot Town Death Trip" series in the *Rag*, the tales from *Wicked Washtenaw County* help us to see our place in time: no better, no worse, no different than the tough times suffered by others in this same place a century or more ago. A quarter century after publishing his newspaper series of grisly gore at the railroad tracks, we all cross the intersection of East Cross, North River and the railroad tracks a little more carefully.

Wicked Washtenaw County, too, helps us to examine the quality of our own situation and think beyond the present as we are crossing the tracks of the rest of our lives.

Tom Dodd, editor
Depot Town Rag, Ypsilanti, Michigan, 2010

Acknowledgements

I wish to say thank you to all those who helped to make this book possible. I am grateful for all the help I received from Al Rudisill, president of the Ypsilanti Historical Society; Gerry Pety, archivist; George Ridenour, who helped fill in some of the blanks; and Derek Spinei. I am also grateful for all the help I received from the student workers at the University of Michigan Microfilm Room at the Grade Library, who put up with my repeated questions as they tried to teach me how the equipment worked. I must also say thank you to Tom Dodd for proofreading the work and for the foreword.

Death of Patrick Dunn

What may have been the first murder committed in Washtenaw County occurred on the morning of April 24, 1843. That morning at about 6:00 a.m., Jacob Vandawarker was on his way from his house to his shop when he heard the report of a gun go off. The sound was off to his right, coming from the Irish settlement of Ann Arbor. Soon after, Vandawarker heard someone shouting as if in distress. He also saw others running in that direction and saw Patrick Dunn walking about, holding his hands to his side, as he shouted, "Murder, murder!" Dunn also shouted, "I am shot," and added that it was Charles Chorr who had shot him. Vandawarker could see Chorr standing his doorway.

At this time, a James Weeks came up and asked Dunn what was the matter. To this Dunn said that he had been shot and he wished someone would keep an eye on Chorr and take care of him. To this Dunn added that he was shot and must die and wanted a place to lie down. He was told he had better go to the house, as he was in front of the place where he lived. Dunn again cried, "Murder," and said that if the Almighty God came down upon him, Charles Chorr had shot him. Then Dunn again added that he must die.

Washtenaw County sheriff Peter Slingerland arrived on the scene between 6:00 and 7:00 a.m. and entered the home of Charles Chorr. There he found Chorr at the breakfast table, and he may have been helping his children at the table. Chorr asked Slingerland if he could finish his breakfast. Slingerland noted that Chorr showed no disposition to get away. He found Chorr quiet and peaceable. There was nothing as far as Slingerland could see that was unusual in his conduct or appearance. In the house, Slingerland found three guns, one of which was a smoothbore rifle. This gun was unloaded and appeared as if it had recently been fired. There was a strong smell of fresh burned powder. Slingerland was handed two bullets found by Vandawarker. Dunn died the next day, about twenty-nine hours after the shooting. Before he died, Dunn made a dying declaration that Chorr had shot him.

"They both have a wife and several children left to mourn this awful occurrence," reported the *Argus* of April 26. "A coroner's inquest was held on the body yesterday and a verdict of willful murder rendered."

Chorr underwent examination before Justice Abel and was committed to the county jail to await trial at the next term of the criminal court.

No one seems to have asked what caused Chorr to shot Dunn, as trouble had been brewing between the two for some time. The simple fact was that Dunn was a bully who enjoyed picking on Chorr. Dunn had a bad reputation; some said they would not have believed anything he said even had Dunn been under oath. Chorr, on the other hand, enjoyed a good reputation as a quiet and peaceable man who was kind to family and other people.

It was on June 21, 1842, when Dunn struck Chorr over the head with a club. Chorr fell to the ground without a stagger and then stood up. He and Dunn walked a short distance before Dunn again struck Chorr over the head with the club. Chorr was sick and confined to his home for more than a month after the assault. Dunn was indicted for assault and battery upon the person of Chorr, but there were delays, and the case never came to trial.

Those who knew Chorr before the assault said he was not the same after. Chorr, it was said by those who knew him, would talk about a dozen things at once. Sometimes, his friends noted, he acted strange. Chorr was constantly annoyed by a ticking noise in his head, and when he labored hard it became a rushing sound. When he stooped, he felt a rushing to his head and a throbbing in it.

Dunn and his son would ask Chorr about the watch in his head and if he could tell time by it. Chorr said his head always became worse after being so insulted, as there would be an increase in the rushing sound for a day or two after. Sometimes he would have a disagreeable feeling in his head as if his head were too small.

The delay in bringing the case against Dunn also played on his mind. Chorr sometimes talked about getting revenge on Dunn. When still confined to the house because of the assault, he told Marshall W. Stevens, "I'll have satisfaction whether I can get it by law or not, by God, if it costs me my life." Stevens told Chorr not to make such threats. To this, Chorr said, "I don't care a damn, I'll have satisfaction."

The trial of Chorr for the murder of Dunn opened in the district court for the county of Washtenaw on Wednesday, November 15, 1843, with Judge Witherell presiding. The prosecuting attorney was Edward Mundy, who would also testify as a witness. Mundy told how Chorr was vexed at the delay in taking Dunn to trial for the assault. Chorr had also called on Mundy to make a complaint against the children of Dunn for annoying his family, particularly in his absence. He told Mundy they were throwing chips against the door and calling his wife "hard" names. In his visits, said Mundy, Chorr appeared rational and sane.

Among the witnesses was a Dr. Schetterly, who had treated Chorr after the assault and had seen him a few times after. He was asked, "From the facts given in evidence in this case was there any thing which constituted evidence of insanity?"

Dr. Schetterly answered, "Decidedly thinks so."

A summary of the testimony was published by the *Michigan State Journal* on November 29, 1843, and recorded Dr. Schetterly's response as:

> *If an impression upon a person thinking his best friends who have always treated him as such, for his worst enemies, is not a symptom of insanity, witness don't know what is. Another reason was Chorr's enmity against his sister without any seeming cause. Another reason was his wandering while in conversation with Mrs. Fuller (who had visited Chorr in jail and found him changed). Another is a total change of character as stated with regard to conversation, business &c. These constitute in the mind of witness evidence of symptoms of monomania is sufficient to disqualify Chorr from judging as to right or wrong in regard to his own actions—not to prevent his pursuing his usual work. May have been able to conduct every other business rationally and still be a monomaniac with respect to this difficulty with Dunn. Witness firmly believes that Chorr was insane at the time he conversed with witness at his house.*

At the trial, other doctors testified their opinion that Chorr was sane, and other witnesses told of his having an interest in criminal cases where a defendant was free on the grounds of insanity.

After arguments of counsel, the case was submitted to the jury by the court on the afternoon of Saturday, November 25. That evening, the jury returned a verdict of "guilty of murder in the first degree." Judge Witherell sentenced Chorr to death by hanging. General Edward Clark, who was in command of the militia, was asked to furnish a detachment to be present at the execution. There would be no execution, as Chorr escaped from the county jail and was never seen or heard from again.

Pathways to Freedom

The Underground Railroad in Washtenaw County

S everal lines of the Underground Railroad are known to have passed through Washtenaw County, where fugitive slaves received aid as they made their way from the South to freedom in Canada. Sadly, most of what is known of the Underground Railroad is myth. After the Civil War, when having taken part in the Underground Railroad was safe and prestigious, many came forward with their tales of bravery and daring-do, and some of the stories were true.

Even now, when an old house or building is being remodeled and what might have been a hidden room is found, the assumption is made that it was part of the Underground Railroad. Some of these houses and buildings were built long after the Civil War but before Prohibition.

The Underground Railroad was described as "a railroad, but with no time table, no tickets, no fares, no president, no regularly organized company, no definitely laid out route. Conductors it had and stations, but their names were kept a secret." In truth, only a few were part of the Underground Railroad, and some of these conductors lived in Washtenaw County.

There was a reason for those active in the Underground Railroad to keep it secret. What they were doing was illegal and dangerous. Under the Fugitive Slave Act of September 18, 1850, anyone who helped a slave escape could be fined $1,000 and jailed for up to six months. Appointed commissioners would decide if those accused of being runaway slaves should be returned to their owners or freed. Those accused of being runaway slaves had no right of counsel, could not testify on their own behalf and were denied right of trial by jury. Commissioners were paid $10 for each slave returned to their owner and $5 for each person freed.

After the passage of the Fugitive Slave Act, escaped slaves who had settled in the North feared being returned to slavery. Because of this fear, many fled to Canada, and stories were told of whole communities of African Americans who had crossed the border, some with only the clothes on their backs.

Mary A. Goddard, assistant professor of natural sciences at the Michigan State Normal College, now Eastern Michigan University, researched the Underground Railroad in Ypsilanti for a paper she gave in April 1913. She wrote:

> *Even the children of the families of those connected with it knew little of what was actually going on about them. The success of the institution depended on secrecy. So it happened that many of the leading workers died without having told even their children much, if anything, about their activities in the Underground Railroad. Some who may yet be living are unknown, and it is not easy to search them out. In these investigations many people have been visited, but few have been able to give any information, though they were living in Ypsilanti at the time when the work of the Railroad was at its height.*

As part of her investigation, Mary Goddard interviewed Anna McCoy, the daughter of George McCoy. George McCoy was born a slave, the property of his father, in Louisville, Kentucky. At the age of twenty-one, George was freed and given a horse, saddle and $100, but he stayed with his father, working in his father's cigar shop. George married a woman named Mildred, a slave belonging to a family named Gaines. The two fled to Canada, where they settled for some time. Then the family moved to Ypsilanti. The family lived for a time on the farm of John and Maryann Starkweather. George grew tobacco and made cigars, which he sold in Wyandotte and Detroit.

Mary Goddard wrote:

> *Mrs. McCoy remembers, when she was little, going to the post office for mail. Sometimes letters would come from a Mr. Hatfield of Cincinnati. On*

these days her mother would bake a large batch of bread and cook hams. Then the children would be put to bed early, being told it was good for children to get plenty of sleep. The next day her father would always make a trip. As Anna grew older, she noticed that shortly after they went to bed the smell of coffee pervaded the house, and the following day little would be left of the large baking. These things, together with her Father's trips, seemed very mysterious and greatly aroused her curiosity, but by degrees, as she grew older, she discovered what it was all about.

George carried the escaping slaves in the false bottom of his covered wagon. At Wyandotte, a Mr. Bush aided the slaves' escape to Canada in his boat, the *Pearl*. It is not known how much John and Maryann Starkweather knew of what George was doing.

Another who is known to have been active in the Underground Railroad was Leonard Chase, who ran a station from his home on Cross Street in Ypsilanti, one block east of the Huron River, although some sources place the house near the present site of the water tower. Mrs. Eunice Lambie Hatch recalled her grandmother, Mrs. Maria Morton, preparing food and carrying the food to the Chase home. The Hatch home was on River Street and was demolished in the 1960s.

A family named Prescott lived in a log cabin near where the Peninsular Paper Mill stood, now the site of Peninsular Place Apartments. They were abolitionists and conductors in the Underground Railroad. Mrs. Prescott ran a school for African American children in their home. Anna McCoy was one of her students.

Prince Bennett was a Quaker who lived south of Ypsilanti in Augusta Township. The house stood on Tuttle Hill Road, a half mile north of Willis Road. Bennett is said to have had a hidden room under his porch, covered with a trapdoor. A rug was placed over the trapdoor and a rocking chair set on the rug.

One day, slave catchers came by and asked Bennett's wife, who was sitting in the rocking chair, if she had seen any escaped slaves. She gave an honest answer of "No." She had not seen any slaves that day, as they were in the hidden room under her rocking chair. The Bennett house is said to have burned down early in the twentieth century.

Those who lived in the northern states were for the most part opposed to slavery for many reasons. Some saw slavery, the ownership of another human being, as a moral evil. Others opposed slavery for reasons of economic self-interest, as they did not want to be in competition with cheaper slave labor.

The Prince Bennett home in Augusta Township. *Used with permission of the Ypsilanti Historical Society.*

Conductors of the Underground Railroad had to keep their actives secret, even from fellow abolitionists who may have seen aiding escaping slaves as a moral wrong. After all, at that time slavery was legal and slaves were the rightful property of their owners. Helping slaves escape could be seen as no better than theft.

One in Ypsilanti who knew the evil of slavery from firsthand experience was "Dick" Johnson, who was the porter at the Hawkins House Hotel for many years. He was born a slave on a plantation in Virginia, where he lived the life of a person considered to be goods and chattel of another.

> *For trivial offenses, many of which arose from his ignorance, he was beaten until the blood poured down his back in streams, and he was made to fell that he was the veriest scum of the earth, with not a single right or feeling that should be respected. He had not the slightest knowledge of the books or of the world, the universe for him consisting of his master's plantation and a few miles of country in four directions.*

At the age of seventeen, Johnson was taken by his owners to Washington, D.C., as a servant to see the inauguration of President James Buchanan. Traveling in separate railroad cars, Johnson lost track of his owners. After wandering about for hours, he boarded a train that was pulling out of the station. He made his way to Ohio, where he was aided by the Underground Railroad to travel to Detroit and from there to Windsor.

"Johnson tells of a visit to his old home some years after the war," reports an undated account from the *Ypsilanti Daily Press* in the files of the Ypsilanti City Archive, "and how his mother did not recognize him when he stopped at her house and asked for shelter for the night, and how she fainted for joy when he finally revealed his identity." The family tried to find a sister who had been sold by their owners but were never able to learn her fate.

Slaves escaping from the South had to rely on their own courage and ingenuity to stay alive and avoid capture. Fugitive slaves did not receive aid from the Underground Railroad until after passing into the Free States. They had to make the most risky part of the trip on their own. Even in the Free States, fugitive slaves were still at risk of capture.

Fugitive slaves often traveled from Ohio to Blissfield, Adrian, Clinton, Ann Arbor, Ypsilanti, Plymouth, Belleville, Wartsburg and finally Detroit. Once in Detroit, the fugitive slaves were taken across the river to Canada. Travel was often made at night under the cover of darkness. Sometimes lanterns were hung from barns to guide fugitive slaves to a safe house. At other stations, someone would lead the fugitive slaves to the next station or convey them in some transport such as a wagon with a false bottom. The stations of the Underground Railroad were often ten miles apart and managed by volunteers. At the stations, the escaping slaves were provided with shelter, food, clothing and, if necessary, medical care. At Ypsilanti, Dr. Helen McAndrew, the first female doctor in Washtenaw County, is said to have provided assistance to fugitive slaves.

A station of the Underground Railroad was operated at the Chubb farm in Wayne County at the junction of Elm Road and Michigan Avenue for many years. An account of the operation of the station was provided to the *Ypsilanti Daily Press* for a story published on Monday, November 24, 1919, by Henry W. Barnard, who married one of the Chubb daughters and took part in the station's operation. The account begins:

It is a dark night. The stars are hidden by low hanging clouds and a summer rain is beating threateningly against the windows as Mr. and Mrs. Chubb and the three daughters are busily engaged indoors in completing what has been a hard day's work. The three boys are not at home and an inquiry as to their whereabouts would have brought some evasive answer. Had you been present you would have observed nothing more or less than a typical country homestead scene.

As the time passes, the family becomes more anxious as some growing concern causes the family to stay up past their usual bed time.

An unusually heavy crash of thunder following a brilliant flash across the sky and Chubb turns from the window. No words are spoken but in the hearts of the mother and daughters is an understanding that prefaces speech. Going into the kitchen the father prepares to go out into the storm while the daughters seem to be starting the preparation of a meal. The mother has just finished placing a fire under the kettle when the creaking of a wagon is heard outside and there is the soft whinnying of a horse coming more faintly from the direction of the stable.

The door opens and closes and the mother and daughters pause in mute questioning during the few seconds before the sound of splashing footsteps is overcome by the noise of the storm.

Within a few minutes lunch has been prepared and stands awaiting upon the kitchen table. There is a steaming pail of tea, some generous slices of tempting cold boiled ham: a pile of bread spread thick with golden butter; and some of those old-fashioned tarts—the fluffy kind with crabapple jelly in the center. The tray is piled high.

Quietly the door opens and Chubb shakes the water from his dripping clothes.

The mother glances anxiously at his face.

"Four, Mother," in answer to her silent questioning. "Father, mammy and two children, one a little pickaninny about two years old."

To the supply on the tray is added a bowl of milk.

"From Louisiana," continues Chubb. "Carter brot them from the station below underneath a covering of hay. Been five hours on the way and bad going too. Rained all the way but that helped as they met no one. Guess they will be safe above the cow manger, until the boys get back and can get them over the river."

Relieved at the information and with the knowledge of that little pickaninny waiting for the bowl of milk, Mrs. Chubb places the tray in the father's arms. Her first duty to the refugees is finished.

The next day, the Chubb boys hid the fugitives in a wagon covered with loose straw or hay and transported them to a safe place in Detroit where a rowboat was waiting to carry the family across the river to freedom. Care had to be taken, as slave catchers traveled throughout the North including Washtenaw and Wayne Counties, hunting for fugitive slaves. It is little wonder then that those active in the Underground Railroad kept their activities secret from family, friends and neighbors.

Fugitive slaves were welcomed in Canada in part because large portions of the country were unsettled. As the land was cleared, the fugitive slaves were a source of labor, and many of them had knowledge of agriculture. The fugitive slaves carried with them the technique of curing tobacco, which was raised and exported beginning in the 1840s. "Along the lakefront," wrote Mary Goddard, "white settlers were opening up clearings, and farm hands were hard to get. Consequently when the penniless slaves came, eager to earn money, they were warmly received."

Sylvester D. Noble was a conductor in Ann Arbor for many years. He lived on Chapin Street just off West Huron at the foot of what was called "Piety Hill." His daughter, Pamela Noble, recalled a number of fugitive slaves coming to the house and being fed and cared for. Mary Goddard wrote:

Two escaped slaves George and Martha Washington lived for a long time in a little house near the Nobles. They did gardening and other work for Mr. Noble. One night after dark some of the children of the family were sent across the "Chapin lot" with a basket of food for the Washington family. They found a number of people there, hurrying to get George and Martha off to Canada. The "Fugitive Slave Law" had just been passed and a rumor had reached them that the master of George and Martha was coming for them. Although little was said to the children of the family, Miss Noble remembers, aside from this incident, that people were sometime hidden in their cellar. The hidings were always followed by mysterious journey by her father. Once she remembers he had two men in the back of his wagon and a woman on the seat with him. He took fugitive slaves either to or away from the home of a Mr. Lowry of Lodi.

Capitan John Lowry. *From Chapman's* History of Washtenaw County.

Captain John Lowry of Lodi Township felt that it was better to please God than to please man and worked for the common good. Chapman's *History of Washtenaw County*, published in 1881, noted that Lowry was considered eccentric by many. Chapman's history notes that many of the "bloodhound-hunted children of our common father often found rest and comfort in Captain Lowry's well-stored home, where much money and clothing were given to supply the wants of the escaped slaves."

Lowry was outspoken in his opposition to slavery, a point of view shared by many of those who settled on the land near his home. He expressed his wish that slavery and oppression end by erecting a sign on large boards on poles near his home. His daughter, Mary Foster, read a paper to the Pioneer Society of Michigan in 1880, which was published in Volume II, 1880. This is how she described the sign:

> *The figure at the right is a female, with heavy chain in her left hand, but broken are the links. In her right hand she holds a balances; to the left, and in the act of rising, is the figure of a man of darker hue, and lips so thick and hair like wool, but clad in freeman's garb, while around one wrist is clasped the other end of slavery's chain, with many missing links, and to his sister, he looks up for help and perfect freedom their faces all aglow with triumph, and just below appears this motto: "Liberty to the fugitive captive and the oppressed over all the earth, both male and female of all colors."*

One who shared the sentiments of Lowry, if in a quieter manner, was Asher Aray, an African American of mixed descent living in Pittsfield Township. Jacob Aray, the father of Asher, settled in the area in 1827 on 160 acres of land near what is now West Michigan Avenue. Asher and his wife, Catherine, settled on property purchased from his father. There the family harbored fugitive slaves as they made their way to Canada. It is said that Aray was aided in this work by the families of William Webb Harwood and Roswell Preston, who lived nearby.

Chapman's *History of Washtenaw County* noted that Roswell Preston

> *deemed a life conscious of righteousness, truth and kindness to the needy and suffering, of greater value than sentiment and zeal that may glitter with the multitude and fail in a trying time. He sought not a showy or brilliant life, but a useful one, and endeared himself to many by kindness without reference to rank or grade of society, and he is said to have been familiar with passengers on that mysterious Underground Railroad. Peace be to his ashes, and useful lives and a bright future to his family.*

There were others who were active in the Underground Railroad in Washtenaw County, but they carried their stories to their graves. They did not seek glory or honor but acted out of a belief of what was right and moral,

Asher Aray. *Used with permission of the Ypsilanti Historical Society.*

often in the face of a majority who opposed them. Those who took part in the Underground Railroad are for the most part forgotten, the courage of their convictions little noted, their deeds of daring covered in secrecy; but that is how they wanted it.

Body Snatching and the University of Michigan

E very year, the medical school of the University of Michigan is ranked among the top ten of such institutions in the nation, bringing prestige to the university and the surrounding community. The medical school of the University of Michigan is a source of pride to students, faculty and the community. This was not always the case, however, as in the early years of the medical school, it was a source of shame and infamy. The reason for this was the need of the medical school for cadavers, dead bodies, for the study of anatomy. To have enough cadavers for the students to study, the school had to deal in body snatching.

A doctor must have an understanding of human anatomy, and the only way to acquire such knowledge is by the dissection of a human body. A medical student must spend time taking a human body apart to study the internal organs to come to an understanding of how the body works. For this reason, medical schools had to have an adequate supply of cadavers on hand for the students to study. The problem for medical schools in the nineteenth century and into the early years of the twentieth, including the one at the University of Michigan, was how to obtain the necessary number of cadavers every year. This was not an easy problem to solve, as public feeling in America called for respect for the body of a deceased loved one, and this meant that the body should receive proper burial in a cemetery. The idea of turning a body over to a medical school, such as the one at the University of Michigan, was repugnant to most Americans.

The Michigan legislature passed a law in 1838 that made grave robbing illegal and provided a heavy fine and a term of one-year imprisonment for those who were convicted. The medical profession in 1844 proposed that the legislature make it legal for prison wardens to deliver the dead bodies of prisoners to the medical school of the University of Michigan, should it be established. One member of the legislature referred to the proposal as "a bill to appropriate the bodies of the poor for the benefit of science." Another member of the legislature sarcastically called it "a bill…to prevent physicians from robbing graveyards." The bill was passed, but the supply of cadavers was still inadequate. The prison population of the state was small, and in 1846, capital punishment was abolished in the state of Michigan. Professors of anatomy and their students still found themselves forced to visit the local graveyard at night to dig up a body and stealthily carry it off. In time, professionals arrived on the scene, those willing to carry out the grisly and sometimes dangerous work…for a price.

The first thing a good grave robber had to do was know when a body was available for snatching. The body had to be snatched as soon after the burial as possible, usually the first night after the funeral. The body had to be disinterred before the process of decomposition had set in and while the ground was still loose. The robber had to find the location of the grave during the day so as to prevent stumbling around a cemetery at night. A grave robber would arrive at a cemetery during the funeral dressed as a hunter after small game. He would take note of the location of the grave and any landmarks nearby to facilitate finding it in the dark. Rural cemeteries were preferred, the ones far from the city or town, with no one living near who might see the robbers at work and sound the alarm.

Grave robbing was a three-man operation. One man was to drive the wagon needed to convey the body. He would drop off the other two and then drive off to return at a set time. They dared not park the wagon in or near the cemetery, as this was cause for suspicion if seen. Grave robbers did not like their work to be interrupted by angry mobs looking to rip them apart limb from limb.

"Two able bodied men were needed to make the disinterment," wrote Frederick C. Waite in "Grave Robbing in New England," published in *Bulletin of the Medical Library Association,* July 1945.

The entire surface of the grave was carefully examined with a shaded lantern on arrival. A common practice was for some friend of the deceased to arrange in the closed grave a careful pattern of stones, shells, sticks, or flowers in order to detect disturbance. This pattern had to be mapped so that it could be restored exactly after the disinterment.

Two large tarpaulins were necessary parts of the equipment. One was spread beside the grave and all the excavated soil thrown upon it so that when this soil was returned to the grave there should be no telltale bits left on the grass. Inasmuch as in each cemetery all burials were with the head in a certain direction, the position of the head of the grave could be determined by neighboring tombstones.

The grave robbers made an excavation of approximately three square feet at the head of the grave until they reached the coffin. This was usually at a depth of four feet or less, so they had no more than thirty-five cubic feet of soil to handle. This was an easy task, as the soil was loose.

Now the grave robbers had to open the coffin, using an auger to bore a row of holes at the head end of the coffin. They did not use a saw or axe, as the noise would be risky. Opening the coffin was an easy matter.

The grave robbers would then use a tool known as "the hook," a strong iron bar five feet long with one end turned up into a blunt hook of about two inches. They placed the hook under the chin of the body and pulled it from the coffin and onto a tarpaulin previously lain at the head of the grave. Then the body was stripped of the shroud and any other apparel, which was then tossed back into the coffin. This was necessary as clothing would make identification of the body possible if discovered. The body was then wrapped in the tarpaulin so nothing could drop from the body, such as a personal item, like a ring, onto the ground, leaving evidence of the grave having been disturbed.

Waite continued:

The body having been wrapped, the excavated soil was returned to the grave and the surface carefully restored to the exact condition in which it had been found. Next all tools were counted and wrapped in the tarpaulin upon which the soil had been thrown and the tarpaulin securely tied so that no tool could drop out. This gave only two bundles which two able-bodied men could carry to the waiting conveyance in one trip.

Waite noted that two able-bodied men could complete a disinterment in one hour from the time they entered the cemetery until the time they left the cemetery. He also noted that if the grave robbers followed each of these steps, it was unlikely the disinterment would be discovered. The grave robbers then had to delivery the body to the medical school. In the early years of the nineteenth century, the medical school could be no more than fifteen miles from the cemetery. The body had to be delivered before daylight, when someone might notice suspicious activity at the school. Once the body was safe at the school, the janitor would pay the grave robbers and hide the body.

Steps were taken through the years to prevent the theft of bodies, such as placing heavy stones over the coffin or placing the body in a vault on the grounds of the cemetery until the process of decay had set in. Some families would employ someone to stand guard over the grave through the night, every night, until it was no longer of interest to robbers. Sometimes a warning shot from a watchman frightened off would-be grave robbers. A watchman, however, was expensive and was an option available only to the wealthy. A watchman could also be bribed or supplied with whiskey by grave robbers so he would sleep through the whole operation. When a member of a church community died, sometimes the men of the community would take turns standing watch over the grave every night until the body was no longer marketable. Somehow, it seemed, the grave robbers were able to overcome every obstacle.

When a disinterment was discovered and publicized, the public reaction was outrage and indignation. Sometimes a mob would gather to storm the nearest medical school. On a few occasions, the school building was damaged or even destroyed. When, in 1852, the remains of a young woman were found in a cesspool attached to Cleveland's homeopathic medical college, the building was stormed by a mob. They smashed some sixty windows, destroyed the museum and laboratory and set fire to the building.

In the 1850s, a grave was found to have been desecrated in Jackson County, Michigan, and the body traced to the medical school at the University of Michigan in Ann Arbor. The reaction to the news of this was, predictably, public outrage and indignation. At one Ann Arbor saloon, the men, once well fortified with drink, decided to burn down the medical school building. Among those in the saloon at the time were some medical school students who hurried to the campus and rallied their fellow students to action. The students organized patrols armed with guns and clubs and stood ready to face off the mob. The mob, realizing the force they faced, returned to the saloon to reconsider their course of action and ordered another round. The medical school building was safe.

The Medical School building was made in the style of a Greek temple with columns and portico, and it was once the most handsome on campus. Built in 1850, it was demolished in 1914. *Used with permission of the Bentley Historical Library, University of Michigan.*

The Medical School of the University of Michigan opened on the first Wednesday of October in 1850. Anatomy was one of the courses offered. At this time the school only needed fifteen to twenty cadavers every year, and the catalogue of the university made no mention of "anatomical material." Practical anatomy was made a requirement for graduation in 1852. This was the first laboratory course at the university required for graduation. The catalogue of 1852–53 has a short sentence stating the school had an adequate supply of anatomical material.

The number of students enrolled in the medical school during the first years was small. This changed after the Civil War, when discharged veterans enrolled in the school, bringing the number of students in 1866–67 up to 525. Now the school needed 125 cadavers, and that meant body snatching.

At about this time a Dr. Ford, professor of anatomy, wrote a letter to Regent Gilbert about "the material wants of the Department of Anatomy." To find the supply of cadavers, Dr. Ford explained, the demonstrator of

The medical faculty and students of the medical school in 1865. The increased enrollment that followed the Civil War resulted in a need for more cadavers. *Used with permission of the Bentley Historical Library, University of Michigan.*

anatomy had to travel 1,200 to 1,500 miles a year. This was necessary because he realized the need to keep the peace in the Ann Arbor area, so he filled the department's needs by finding the cadavers somewhere else. Grave robbing was an undignified profession, Dr. Ford noted, but it was necessary for the advancement of medicine.

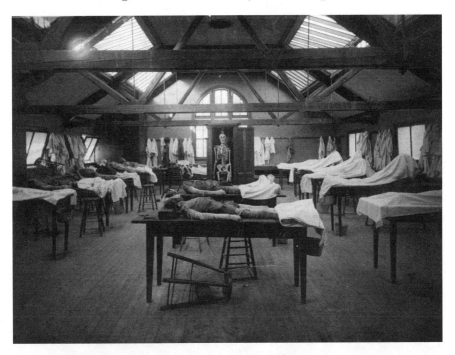

The anatomical laboratory where the cadavers were kept and dissections were carried out. *Used with permission of the Bentley Historical Library, University of Michigan.*

"He cannot go into the field in strange places," wrote Dr. Ford. "He must find men willing to undertake such illegal and dangerous work; they have been bribed and they are not reliable. Money must be spent; arrangements to escape detection must be made. After a body is received it must be boxed, carted, and transported, all by unreliable persons who must be bribed." The demonstrator must have been resourceful, as he had a network of twenty to thirty people who kept the department well supplied. "I can inform you," wrote Dr. Ford in conclusion, "as one of us of which as my obvious reasons we keep sacredly (not just secretly) to ourselves, even some of my colleagues do not know of our danger."

One who understood the danger was Dr. George E. Frothingham, demonstrator of anatomy, who wrote a letter to the regents dated March 11, 1869, to ask for a raise in salary. One reason Dr. Frothingham felt he deserved a raise was the difficulty he faced in obtaining cadavers. Dr. Frothingham explained that he "was compelled to violate the laws of several states, and was, therefore, in constant danger of being disgraced, by detection, arrest and imprisonment." He constantly had to travel "in the dark nights" to unfrequented parts of strange cities, either alone or in company with those whose presence, in many cases, "only added to the feeling of insecurity." Dr. Frothingham informed the regents that of the previous winter's supply of cadavers, "not one subject could be obtained in any legal manner."

Among those who supplied the medical school with cadavers were a Mr. Hill, his son and another man. Mr. Hill died and was buried. The next day, the son of Mr. Hill and the other man arrived at the medical school with the body of Mr. Hill, ready to advance the cause of medicine.

On September 7, 1876, the James-Younger gang rode into Northfield, Minnesota, planning to hold up the bank. The holdup did not go as planned, as the citizens of the town shot and killed two of the gang members and wounded others. One of the gang members was shot and killed by Howard Wheeler, a student at the medical school at the University of Michigan.

The first women were admitted to the medical school in the fall of 1870, and they, too, had to take part in the dissection of cadavers. *Used with permission of the Bentley Historical Library, University of Michigan.*

That night, as Wheeler was riding with the posse after the gang, Clarence E. Persons, also a student at the medical school, exhumed the two bodies, placed each in a keg marked "Fresh Paint" and had them shipped to Ann Arbor. Friends of one of the outlaws arrived at Ann Arbor and demanded the body be turned over to them. This was done, but Wheeler and Persons dissected the other.

The *Detroit Evening News* of Monday, January 21, 1878, reported that Officers Hughes and Keip of Toledo, Ohio, had been in Ann Arbor searching for the bodies of Mrs. Mary Liener and Charley Ball, which had been exhumed from a cemetery in Toledo on Monday of the week before. The report noted that three men, called Messrs Morton Brother & Co., consisting of Charles P. and Henry Morton and a man named Beverlie, also known as Johnson, were under arrest and charged with the offense.

The account stated:

> *When arrested Henry Morton "squealed," when the balance of the "firm" confessed to having shipped the bodies to the Michigan University. The bodies arrived Wednesday afternoon, and Thursday night the officers came. They took a look through the medical college and found the objects of their search. Demonstrator Herdman says he knows nothing of the manner in which the objects were procured, and he is believed. Last night the officers left in the late train, taking with them the bodies.*

On about April 1, 1878, a John Jackwert died at the almshouse at Erie, Pennsylvania, and was buried. A few days later, a warden of the cemetery discovered that the grave had been disturbed. Upon further investigation, it was found that the body was gone. Thomas Crowley, the chief of police of Erie, was informed, and shortly after he learned that a box that was said to contain fish had been shipped from Erie on April 3 to Ypsilanti, Michigan. The box was to be delivered to a W.H. Stevens of Ypsilanti. Chief Crowley telegraphed the police in Ypsilanti, who found that the address had been changed to W.H. Stevens, Ann Arbor, and sent there. This information was sent to Washtenaw County sheriff Josiah S. Case, who received it Friday night.

The *Ann Arbor Register* of Wednesday, April 10, 1878, reported:

> *He found that the box had been delivered at the Medical College, and on Saturday visited Dr. Herdman, Demonstrator of Anatomy, and stated*

that the body had been traced to the college, and requested Dr. Herdman to see that it was left undisturbed until someone arrived to identify it. Mr. Crowley arrived here on Saturday, at midnight, and Sheriff Case and he went to the Medical College on Sunday, when the body was identified and arrangements made for shipping it back to Erie on Monday.

The express agent at Erie informed Chief Crowley that similar boxes had been shipped from Erie to different localities for the previous four years, but there had been no suspicion of body snatching before.

The *Ann Arbor Courier* of Friday, April 12, 1878, opined:

We trust that the next legislature of the State will see the necessity of making provisions for supplying the medical colleges with the bodies of all paupers and criminals not claimed by the relatives, and thus cure their squeamishness in dealing with this subject. As long as medical colleges exist, so long they will obtain subjects if they are not supplied to them

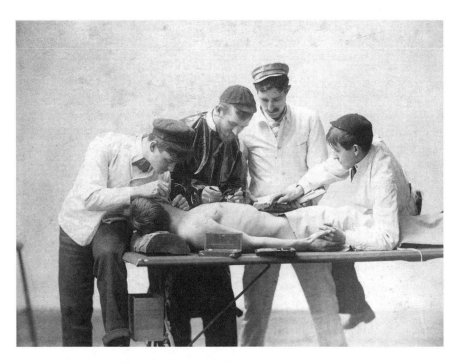

Students carry out a dissection on a cadaver in the anatomical laboratory. *Used with permission of the Bentley Historical Library, University of Michigan.*

willingly, there will always be found plenty of men who, for pecuniary reward, will engage in the ghostly business of desecrating graves.

John Scott Harrison died in his seventy-fourth year in May 1878 at North Bend, Ohio. He was the son of former president William Henry Harrison and father of future president of the United States Benjamin Harrison. Because North Bend was only twelve miles from Cincinnati, where several medical colleges were in operation, the family had taken precautions to prevent the body from being stolen. These precautions included the placing of the coffin in a cement vault set in the grave and covering the casket with a heavy stone. A night watchman was employed to stand guard over the grave for a week after the funeral.

During the Harrison funeral, it was noticed that the grave of a young man named Augustus Devin, who had died the week before, had been disturbed. Friends of Devin set out for Cincinnati after the funeral in hope of recovering the body. A search warrant was procured, and the search for the body started the next afternoon. The search began at the Ohio Medical College.

The *New York Times* of Friday, May 31, 1878, reported:

Before proceeding to the search the party was joined by John Harrison, son of the man buried yesterday, who came up from North Bend this morning with the intention of aiding his friends in their efforts to recover the stolen corpse. The college is not now in session, and few bodies were found in the dissecting rooms. None of those examined bore any resemblance to the remains of the young man, and the party were about leaving the building when young Harrison noticed a windlass with a rope reaching down to the lower story. Pulling at this he discovered that at the other end of the rope a human body was tied. The body was drawn up and a cloth removed from the face, when the horror-stricken youth instantly recognized the features of his father, whose grave he had left but a few hours before. The long beard had been cut off and the body otherwise disguised, but all doubts as to its identity were soon removed by the arrival from North Bend of Carter Harrison, another son of the deceased, with the news that the grave had been robbed during the night.

The janitor was arrested, and the college denied any part in body snatching. The body of Devin was traced to Ann Arbor, where a search was made. At the medical college, they examined the bodies and finally found Devin. They made an affidavit that this was the body of Devin at the request of Dr. William J. Herdman. Dr. Herdman refused to release the body until he was paid thirty dollars as reimbursement for the payment he had made to the grave robbers. The family refused and threatened legal action. The body was finally released by order of James T. Angell, president of the University of Michigan.

The *Ann Arbor Courier* of Friday, June 21, 1878, reported:

> *It is the intention of this department to procure the bodies of paupers, and from potters' field, which have no friends. Their employees who procure bodies have their instructions to do this, but it sometimes happens that some unscrupulous ones exceed their instructions, which results in cases of this kind. We are glad to state that such instances are rare, however. Bodies must be had for anatomical purposes, but the rule of the department is to take no bodies from the vicinity of the college.*

This was followed by the strange case of Dr. Bash of Indianapolis, who arrived at Ann Arbor on Saturday, June 29, 1878, in search of the body of his brother. Dr. Bash arrived with a Cincinnati detective named Colonel Snelbaker, and the two obtained a warrant from Justice Clark to search the medical college. Dr. Bash said that his brother Jonathan had died on June 8, 1878, but when the grave of the brother was later examined, the body was gone. Dr. Bash further said that he had not told anyone of the theft, so as to spare the feelings of family and friends. After the discovery of the body of Devin at the University of Michigan, he decided to search in the same place. He and Detective Snelbaker searched the medical college on Saturday night and Sunday morning, where they found the remains of Jonathan Bash, the deceased brother.

The body was taken to the rooms of a Mr. Martin on Main Street, where it was prepared for shipment back to Indianapolis. Detective Snelbaker left on an early train Sunday morning, while Dr. Bash prepared to leave the same day on the 2:00 p.m. train with the body of his brother. Just before Dr. Bash boarded the train, he was handed a telegram stating that there had to be a mistake. The telegram informed Dr. Bash that the grave of his brother had not been disturbed and the body of Jonathan rested in its proper place.

Dr. Bash instructed Mr. Martin to reconvey the body back to the medical college. He further promised to pay Mr. Martin for this additional trouble. He had already paid Mr. Martin for preparing the body for shipment. Then Dr. Bash boarded the train and left Ann Arbor without further explication.

As Dr. Bash was searching for what he would think was the body of his brother on Saturday, July 5, 1878, a man named Krug, his son and an officer named Scott arrived searching for two missing bodies. They were in search of the body of Mr. Krug's daughter, who had drowned at Logansport, Indiana, on February 24, 1878.

"Some four weeks after the death of his daughter he and his wife were visiting the grave when they noticed that the head of the grave had sunk a foot or so," reported the *Ann Arbor Register* of Wednesday, July 10, 1878. "They also noticed that the grave near by of the man who had been killed by the railroad accident, presented the same appearance." Nothing was done at that time, but this was recalled after the discovery of the body of Devin at the University of Michigan. The two graves were opened and found to be empty.

The books of the express company showed that a box had been sent from Logansport to Ann Arbor and delivered to the medical college on February 26. From the weight of the box, it was supposed that it contained the remains of Mr. Krug's daughter and the remains of the man killed in the railroad accident. After their arrival at Ann Arbor, the three consulted with Sheriff Case, who advised them to see Dr. Dunster, who said Sheriff Case would render them all the necessary facilities for a search without a warrant.

The account noted:

> Sheriff Case and the three gentlemen called upon Dr. Dunster and were assured by him that all bodies which had been received here in February had been used upon the dissecting tables, as the college had run out of material after that date. But to further convince Mr. Krug that his daughter's remains were not here, Dr. Dunster took him to the Medical College and the bodies in the vaults were examined. Mr. Krug, seeing that he had arrived too late to recover the body, if indeed it had ever been sent here as he supposes, took the first afternoon train and returned to Logansport.

The *Ann Arbor Courier* received a letter from someone who seemed to hold an informed opinion on the subject of body snatching and the need for cadavers for dissection at the medical college. This letter to the editor was published in full on the front page of the *Ann Arbor Courier* on Friday, August 9, 1878. The author of the letter opened by noting that the problem of body snatching existed because the law failed to provide the medical schools with an adequate supply of cadavers for study. The law did provide for obtaining

A corner in the dissecting room where busy students studied the human body by taking it apart. *Used with permission of the Bentley Historical Library, University of Michigan.*

a cadaver by getting the consent of a near relative. This, the author of the letter noted, was easier said than done.

> *The bodies of the friendless in alms houses, prisons, etc., may be obtained by first getting permission of those in charge, and as I understand, it is unlawful to take bodies obtained in this way from one State into another. Were it not for this the surplus in some places might be used to meet the lack of supply in others.*
>
> *A great majority of the people have a particular horror of a dissecting room, and they think it a great insult to the dead to have their bodies appropriated in a manner that they will be of some benefit to the living, so much so that if a physician should be known to possess a private dissecting room, and should be carefully studying the human body to enable him to be more competent to take care of the living ones intrusted to his skill, his orthodox and thoughtless friends would cease to patronize him, and if he were detected in the act of dissecting somebody's friend, he would be branded as a villain, he would be the sole subject for condemnation at the mite societies, and his extremely conscientious creditors would deem*

it a virtue to cheat him out of his just dues. Still, if one of these same Chimpanzees should require a surgical operation from any cause, and the surgeon should fail to make of him a model, he would squirm and twist, and perhaps even swear to a lie to get the last dollar the operator had on earth under a plea of malpractice.

By means of the protracted energy in scientific research of the medical profession, the plagues that once depopulated cities have ceased to visit us. Cholera and smallpox, that made their terrible havoc with human life, have lost their terror, and many who without the aid of the learned treatment of to-day, would be compelled to feel their way through life in utter darkness are made to see, and those who are reaping the benefits of all this are in the background calling the men who work these wonders of science Ghouls, Hyenas, and so on, begrudging them the essential and only material for acquiring a correct knowledge of practical anatomy. They would rather that dead bodies would be dissected by ghastly, wriggling worms than with scalpel and tweezers. The idea that a dead human body should be appropriated to a practical purpose is very abhorrent to them; however it appears all right to put them in the ground as habitation and food for myriads of microscopical animals, which hold their carnivals among the tissues until the skeleton alone remains. They shudder at the thought of a body being found in the University at Ann Arbor, but drink the soakings of a grave yard, without so much as a cannibal "elevation of the nose," and charge up the fatal results to an "inscrutable providence."

A few years before, the author noted, the citizens of Grand Rapids, Michigan, were dying off at such an alarming rate that scientific attention was called in. The problem was drinking water contaminated with poisonous products from a nearby cemetery. How much better, the author committed, for these bodies to have been placed in the "pickling vats" of the medical school or have been cremated. It certainly would have been no worse for the dead.

The author concluded his letter by saying that those who would prevent the medical schools from obtaining bodies for study demanded the benefits of the dissecting table while at the same time doing all in their power to prevent the medical schools from acquiring the necessary supply of cadavers. The author signed his letter "Dissector."

Obtaining a sufficient supply of cadavers was the job of the demonstrator of anatomy at the medical college. In 1880, this post was held by William

The surgery and anatomy class was taught by lectures and demonstrations, but no matter how well done, hands-on experience with the human body was necessary to become a doctor. *Used with permission of the Bentley Historical Library, University of Michigan.*

Herdman, who, in a letter dated June 28, 1880, informed the Board of Regents that he had to commit a number of illegal and unethical acts to secure the ninety to one hundred bodies needed each year. "I have labored early and late and have tested every honorable method," he wrote. He sought to obtain the number needed by legal means first, before resorting to "other means." He assured the Board of Regents that he always tried to obtain the bodies of the "pauper and friendless dead at our county houses and asylums." This, so the better people of the community could rest in comfort. Herdman did not believe it was asking too much that those "unclaimed by friends, cared for by none, useless to himself, be made to contribute to the welfare of his fellows."

To find the cadavers needed, Herdman tried to fulfill the demand that he find these bodies not in Michigan, but in other states. "Gentlemen, by doing so we only rob the graves of our sister states instead of our own."

In order to rob the graves of the sister states, such as Ohio, Herdman told the Board of Regents that he had a spy network so that when a pauper died, Herdman was at once informed. His major problem was to find those willing to secure only the bodies of the paupers and leave the graves of others alone. Those willing to do such work, Herdman observed, were of the lowest character and often disregarded his instructions, robbing the graves of the wealthy as well as the poor. Sometimes, "the intelligence creeps to the surface that an outrage has been committed and that the grave of a respectable citizen has been ruthlessly disturbed." Then, "the University and myself are made the unfortunate victims of their unscrupulous greed."

As it was the practice of Herdman and other demonstrators of anatomy at the university to obtain their bodies from outside the state of Michigan so as to prevent outrage near home, medical schools in other states—for example, Ohio—followed the same practice and obtained their bodies outside their borders, in states such as Michigan. This meant that the body of a person buried in or near Ann Arbor might be safe from the dissecting tables of the University of Michigan, but there was a chance this body could end up on a dissecting table in Ohio.

The problem of body snatching was the result of a lack of laws providing the medical schools with an adequate supply of cadavers for their needs. The first anatomical law passed in the state of Michigan was in 1866, the year Professor Ford wrote his letter to Regent Gilbert. Regent Gilbert was instrumental in passing "an act to authorize dissection in certain cases for the advancement of science." Under this law, bodies were to be supplied from almshouses and courthouses, as well as bodies that would have to be buried at public expense. A body had to be buried, however, if during the last illness the person expressed a wish to be buried. Then the body could not be turned over to a medical school. When the body was that of a stranger to the community where he or she died, then, again, the body had to be buried. This law did little to stop the practice of grave robbing.

An amendment was added to the law in 1871, under which the regents or the faculty could not receive money in excess of the actual cost of the body. Under this amendment, the demonstrator no longer received funds for travel. The idea was to keep the demonstrator in Ann Arbor, and once unable to find those willing to carry out the work of body snatching, the problem of grave robbing, it was thought, would disappear. It did not work out that way.

The Michigan legislature passed Public Act 16 of 1881, which was the first real step to ending the problem of body snatching. Under this act, officials in charge of prisons, jails, hospitals, poorhouses and other institutions that

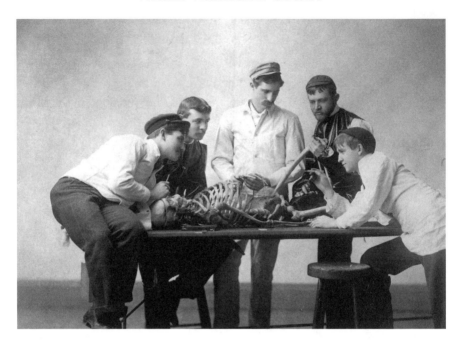

Not much was left of the cadaver after students had completed the dissection. *Used with permission of the Bentley Historical Library, University of Michigan.*

were supported in part or in whole by public funds had to turn over to the medical schools the unclaimed bodies of deceased inmates. Those who failed to comply with the law were to be fined $100 per body.

The problem did not disappear overnight but continued into the next century. The notorious Cantrell gang snatched thousands of bodies from 1890 until 1902 while working in several states. They are known to have sent some of their bodies to medical schools in Michigan, including the University of Michigan. The work of the gang ended in 1902 when the members were arrested in Indianapolis.

The problem of body snatching disappeared from newspapers and public awareness in the early years of the twentieth century. As the supply of cadavers met the needs of the medical schools, the need to steal bodies from the local cemetery vanished. Once the medical schools, including the one at the University of Michigan, had an adequate supply, the market for bodies vanished. Body snatching disappeared from daily life, merged into folk tales and legends and became the stuff of stories told around a campfire or in the late hours of stormy nights.

The Rapalje Riot

Howard Williams, of Muskegon, was a student at the University of Michigan Medical School in the fall of 1878 and was perhaps twenty-one or twenty-two years of age. He had been a student in the Pharmacy Department two years before and was well known among the students of the university and the population of Ann Arbor. Although he attended the laboratory and lectures, it was later said that he was not registered in either department. Williams was rooming at a house on State Street when his death would cause the largest student demonstration in the history of the university up to that time.

On the morning of Wednesday, October 30, 1878, G.R. Clark, a homeopathic student who was rooming in the same house as Williams, stopped by his room to get a match. Clark was surprised to find the door locked. He thought Williams, who had been out the night before, had not returned. He did not think anything was wrong, so he ate his breakfast and went to the university to attend a lecture. Oscar Dorward, a dental student, returned to the house at 9:00 a.m. and tried to open the door to Williams's room. When the door would not open, he tried to unlock it with the key to his own room. When this failed, he put his shoulder to the door and forced it open. On entering the room, Dorward found Williams on the bed, where he lay on his left side with his hand to his mouth, from which had oozed a quantity of froth. The body was warm but lifeless.

On a table was a small morphine bottle with the label scratched off. On the table with the bottle was a glass with traces of a bitter liquid in it. A search of the room failed to turn up a note to explain the act. "Everything in his room was found in neat condition, and his trunk was carefully packed," reported the *Ann Arbor Register* of Wednesday, November 6, 1878.

Coroner Martin Clark was immediately summoned, and he impaneled a jury. A number of witnesses were sworn, and all said that Williams was under some financial trouble. Although he appeared quiet and gentlemanly in his demeanor, he seemed to suffer from some depression, as if he carried a heavy weight on his mind. It was reported that he sometimes opened conversations on the subject of poisons and more than once had hinted at suicide. Once, when talking of morphine he said "that he might take a dose for the purpose of self-destruction."

Williams had arrived at Ann Arbor well provided for financially, but the facts are unclear. His father may have sent him a monthly allowance or given him enough money to cover his needs until Christmas. Williams was extravagant in his expenditures, paying for the wardrobe and other expensive gifts for a certain young woman with whom he was intimate.

A postmortem examination was carried out by Dr. Breakey and Dr. Morton, who found the lungs in a very congested condition, which may have been caused by morphine. "The physicians said that the cause of death was owing to the filling up of the lungs," reported the *Detroit Free Press* of Thursday, October 31, 1878. "But whether this was caused by the taking morphine or not, they could not say without an examination of the stomach."

An effort was made to determine where Williams had obtained the morphine, but nothing definite could be learned. It was found, however, that Williams had been in Tremaine's Drug Store on the Sunday before his death, when someone came in to have a prescription filled. As the clerk was out, Mr. Tremaine would not fill it. Just then, Williams walked in, and as Mr. Tremaine knew that he was well acquainted with drugs, he asked Williams to fill the prescription. Williams agreed, and once the prescription was filled, the customer asked for some morphine pills. Williams found the bottle and handed these to the person as well. Williams might have placed some of the pills in his own pocket at this time.

Jerome Freeman, a barber, testified that on the afternoon of the day before Williams was found dead, Williams had accosted Freeman on the street, requesting a shave, saying, "Come and shave me for the last time."

Freeman assumed that Williams meant he was leaving town, as Williams had said he was going to marry a girl of the city.

"He made quite a confidant of Jerome Freeman, and talked in the most rapturous manner of a girl of the period, named Lou White with whom he was intimate. He freely told of his having purchased her wardrobe and also a fine diamond ring, and that he intended going to Detroit with her upon the day of his death," reported the *Ann Arbor Courier* of Friday, November 1, 1878.

Lou White, also known as Tracy, was employed in a "disreputable house"— that is, a house of prostitution. Williams had stayed in the barbershop all afternoon on the day of his death waiting for her to come. The girl said Williams had visited her at the house on Second Street that evening and had shown her a bottle of morphine and said he was in the habit of taking it. She said he remained at the house until nine o'clock that night. The next day, she said, they were to go to Detroit, where he was to take a position in the perfumery house of J.M. Seely.

The jury rendered the following verdict: "The deceased came to his death from pulmonary congestion produced by an overdose of morphine probably administered by his own hand."

Once the circumstances of the suicide became known, a feeling began to grow among the students of the university, especially among the students of the medical department, that the young woman known as Lou White was the reason for the death of Williams. The feeling was that Williams was so infatuated with the young woman that he spent his money on her, and this caused him to kill himself. The young woman was known to reside in a house on Second Street that was operated by a Mrs. Rapalje, who had been in business for some four or five years. Ann Arbor then had a number of such houses of prostitution seeking the business of the students of the university. Now there grew among the students a feeling that Ann Arbor had one such house too many.

On the morning of Thursday, October 31, 1878, a medical student, while attending a lecture, conceived of the idea of writing a resolution calling the students to take action and "pull" the house. The reasoning of the resolution was that since the young woman, Lou White, had caused Williams to kill himself, the students should break up the house and force the women residing there out of the city. The resolution called on the students to meet at the Leonard House at nine o'clock that evening. The resolution was passed around among the students during the lecture and was well received. The professors learned of the resolution and advised the students to take no illegal action but to let the law take its course. A few of the students assured the professors that they would not take part in any riotous proceedings. The professors were then under the impression that no action would be taken against the house.

Mrs. Rapalje was told of the intent of the students to pull her house and wrote a note to the police requesting protection. She wrote a second note to the professors, asking them to dissuade the students from any such action. The police and the professors, having received the assurances from a few students, were under the impression that the night would pass quietly. They were mistaken.

By 9:00 p.m., a crowd of some six to seven hundred students had gathered in front of the Leonard House. A few minutes after nine, the crowd began to march down Second Street to the house of Mrs. Rapalje, brandishing their various weapons as they did. As the crowd approached the house, Mrs. Rapalje appeared at one of the windows and implored the students to disperse. She said she had nothing to do with the death of Williams and had done nothing to cause such a mob to come and destroy her property and endanger her life.

The crowd of students was not impressed, and two or three of the students constituted themselves into a committee and informed Mrs. Rapalje that she and her five girls were to leave Ann Arbor within twenty-four hours. This she refused to do. On learning this, some of the students began to throw rocks at the house. Some of these rocks crashed through the windows, causing the women in the house to panic and fear for their lives. Those within the house who had revolvers began to fire on the crowd.

The first shot caused the crowd to scatter in all directions without injury. One medical student felt a bullet take a little flesh from his nose and cheek, and another student received a bullet through his hat. After a few minutes, the crowd returned, and an exchange of shots from both sides was kept up for several minutes, with some fifty shots fired. One student fired away at the upper floor of the house with a shotgun, aiming over the heads of his fellow students.

Once the firing had subsided a bit, Mrs. Rapalje again appeared at a window and accepted the terms of the crowd to leave Ann Arbor within twenty-four hours. The two or three police officers who had arrived at the house just after the crowd, but had until now done nothing, came to the front and told the students to leave, as they had achieved their objective. The students returned to the campus, gave three cheers and dispersed.

As the students were returning to the campus, the few police officers on the scene entered the house. Mrs. Rapalje now denied she had entered into an agreement that required her to leave town within twenty-four hours. The police officers handed her a writ of restitution requiring her to leave the house immediately.

The house was, in fact, the property of the Ann Arbor Savings Bank, which came into possession of the house through a mortgage while Mrs. Rapalje was a tenant under a lease from a former owner. The bank sold the house to a resident of Ann Arbor and agreed to give him a bond with the deed when the house was paid for. The man did not occupy the house as the bank expected him to. When the man failed to make the payments, the bank began to take steps to have Mrs. Rapalje evicted from the house. After several months, the writ of restitution was issued a day or two before the students marched on the house.

The march on the house was a topic of conversation among the students for the rest of the week. Notice of a general meeting was passed among the students to be held at 2:00 p.m. the following afternoon. At the appointed hour, some five to six hundred students were present. At the meeting, a Dr. Palmer of the medical department made an appearance, stating that he had come at the request of university president Angel. He told the students he had been assured by Ann Arbor mayor Smith and Sherriff Case that Mrs. Rapalje would leave town as soon as her things were packed. Dr. Palmer advised the students to do nothing more until the following Monday at least, by which time their goal would most likely be accomplished, without their running the risk of being held legally responsible for what he termed their riotous proceedings. "He appealed to them to do nothing in violation of law and order. The speech had a good effect upon the students and the Professor's counsel was accepted," reported the *Ann Arbor Register* of Wednesday, November 6, 1878.

On the morning of the following Monday, the senior class of the medical school held a meeting, at which an attempt was made to pass a resolution condemning those who took part in the action and placing the blame on the junior class. The majority was opposed to this, as it might destroy the good feeling between the classes. The junior class, learning of what the senior class was up to, held a meeting at the same time in another room. A committee was appointed to learn what action the seniors were planning and to, if necessary, draw up resolutions to counteract the false charges.

The *Ann Arbor Register* noted:

> *The truth of the matter is, there were many, both Seniors and Juniors, who took no part whatever in the affair and they think it a little hard they should have to bear a part of the odium. The Juniors held their lyceum on the same evening the riot occurred, did not adjourn until after the assault was made, there were 116 present who did not know there was anything of the kind going on and therefore had nothing to do with it.*

A Dr. Frothingham addressed the medical students on the subject of the riot on Tuesday morning. He told the students that of all his youthful indiscretions, he was proud to say he had never visited such a house. "He considered them as a great blot on our civilization, and wished that they might be swept out of existence, but mob law was not the way to do it. These sudden outbursts of passion were never productive of lasting good, but encouraged a procedure that was subversive of all law and order," reported the *Ann Arbor Courier* of Friday, November 8, 1878.

Dr. Frothingham and a Dr. Maclean, who also spoke, suggested that the students pass resolutions condemning such actions. Such resolutions were passed almost unanimously by the class. The resolutions were:

> *WHEREAS, Certain students in the various departments of this University, in company with rowdies from the city on Thursday evening last, engaged in riotous demonstrations at the house of one Mrs. Rapalje, and*
>
> *WHEREAS, such conduct as was there exhibited tends to the subversion of law and order and the institution of anarchy; therefore*
>
> *Resolved, That as a department we express our entire disapprobation of the acts of mob violence there used, and consider the conduct of those persons who either directly or indirectly instigated or encouraged the riot as reprehensible and deserving of severe censure.*
>
> *Resolved, That deploring as we do the existence of such houses, and knowing them to be a source of disease, immorality and crime, we request the civil authorities to use all proper means for the removal, and keeping of such iniquitous institutions out of the city.*
>
> *By order of the medical class.*

Once this was done, the Rapalje Riot began to fade from memory.

Burning the Normal Organ

Ypsilanti is the home of Eastern Michigan University, established by the Michigan state legislature in 1849 as the Michigan State Normal School. Its first building was dedicated on October 5, 1852.

Harvey C. Colburn in *The Story of Ypsilanti*, published in 1923:

> *The first building of the school was a rectangular, boxlike structure, three stories high and with a flat roof. On the lower floor were rooms for the classes in physics and chemistry, a small reception room, a library, cloak rooms, and a large class room for the model school with desks for eighty-eight pupils. The* [concept of the] *model school did not advance at the time beyond the one-room ideal. On the second floor were the main school room, with seats and desks for two hundred and eight students, and several recitation rooms. The third story contained one room of considerable size and several smaller.*

The Normal building was destroyed by fire on October 28, 1859. The decision was made not to rebuild the structure but to repair the old one. When the work was finished, the school had a sloping roof with a gable over the entrance and a square cupola.

By the 1870s, the accommodations of the building were found to be inadequate, and in 1877, the Michigan state legislature made an

Second Normal School Building. *Used with permission of the Ypsilanti Historical Society.*

appropriation for an addition to the building. This addition was erected on the front of the old building and was eighty-eight feet by ninety-three feet square and three stories high, with a basement. On the third floor of the addition was the chapel.

"The Chapel occupies the entire area of the new building, which is 80x84. The room is 24 feet high, is seated in part with desks, and, as present furnished, will accommodate about 800 persons. The stage is 20x40, and extends 16 feet into the old building," noted the Forty-second Annual Report of the Superintendent of Public Instruction of the State of Michigan for the year 1878.

The *Ypsilanti Commercial* of August 10, 1878, added:

> *The ceiling of the chapel is supported by heavy wood trusses, which add greatly to the furnishing. Three exits enable the large room to be emptied in a very short time. The chapel is so constructed as to be seemingly of good acoustic properties, which probability we trust may be fulfilled for the sake of the youthful orators who will find themselves upon the stage from year to year. The stage, which has*

Addition to the Normal School Building with the chapel in the front of the third floor. *Used with permission of the Archives of Eastern Michigan University.*

a depth of seventeen feet, is connected by double doors with the music room, so that the piano can be readily moved from one to the other.

It was likely believed that a chapel is not complete without an organ. The state board of education purchased a grand organ for the chapel, also known as Normal Hall, in 1886, and the organ was installed in April of that year. This was a grand instrument manufactured by Johnson & Son of Westfield, Massachusetts. This was a two-manual and pedal organ with 1,299 pipes.

No one could have guessed that the organ would almost prove to be the tool of destruction of the Normal building.

Rex Buell was a student in the conservatory at the Normal, and it was his habit to practice on the organ every day from noon to one o'clock. On Saturday, November 11, 1899, Buell entered the chapel through the rear door to see the gleam of fire from the back of the organ. Buell rushed to the narrow passage between the organ and the rear wall of the chapel. There he found the brass pipes of the organ ablaze. The flames were glaring over the top of the instrument and shooting between the pipes. At once, Buell detached a fire hose from its bracket on the wall near the organ and was able to extinguish the flames in a few minutes.

"Had the flames had the right of way for five minutes more, the result may easily be predicted. The material of the organ and woodwork in its vicinity are highly inflammable, and the whole building would probably have been gutted before the flames could have been controlled," noted the *Ypsilanti Commercial* of Thursday, November 16, 1899.

Now the question became, what was the cause of the fire? Arson was suspected at once, as the fire had clearly started at the rear of the organ and near the floor. A wooden stool had been tipped against the organ, and pamphlets had been left in a loose heap about two or three of the pipes and were burning vigorously when discovered by Buell.

A janitor said that he had seen three boys, twelve to fifteen years of age, running down the stairs from the third floor about half an hour before the fire was discovered. At the time, the janitor thought nothing of this, as boys from the training school nearby (now Welch Hall) often found their way into the main building. Buell said as he was approaching the building he had noticed three boys standing on a corner across the street who were looking up at the building with great interest. Neither Buell nor the janitor knew the boys, but each said they could identify them.

"The deed could be attributed to boys on the grounds that it was done by accident while the lads were smoking or playing with matches back of the organ, or that it was committed in a spirit of wanton mischief to see the fire department come out or because they were formerly 'blow boys,' who were taking revenge because their work is now done by the water motor," observed the *Washtenaw Evening Times* of Monday, November 13, 1899. The "blow boys," or bellows boys, were the young men who worked to keep the organ supplied with air while the organ was being played.

The three young boys who had been seen running down the stairs just before the fire was discovered were Clifford Earl, Dode Bell and Robtoy, who was identified in accounts of the case by only the one name, and their ages were fourteen, twelve and ten, respectively. The three were brought before Normal College president Lyman and police officials and denied all knowledge of the fire. They confessed to being in the chapel but said they had done nothing worse than read dime novels. As the three were descending the stairs, the fire developed. Clifford Earl, the fourteen-year-old, returned to the chapel because, he said, he had left his gloves near the organ. Earl swore with the most earnest and innocent countenance that he had not even thought of starting a fire. He added that there had not been the slightest

The Normal chapel with the grand organ. *Used with permission of the Archives of Eastern Michigan University.*

sign of a fire while they were in the chapel. Earl was suspected of being the author of the fire, but as there was no evidence to prove this, no proceedings were instituted.

All the authorities could do was wait and listen. In due time, word reached them that Earl had acknowledged his guilt to a friend. The friend was found and questioned and, after considerable coaxing, said Earl had told him that he was the one who had started the fire. Then Earl was again questioned, and again he remained steadfast in his protestations of innocence. Earl said his friend had lied about what he had said.

Then Deputy P.W. Ross questioned Earl. Officer Ross opened the questioning with the statement: "Of course I know your part in the fire, but now I want you to tell me about the other two boys. What did they do? Did they help you?"

At this, Earl once again protested his innocence in the most earnest tones, claiming he had nothing to do with starting the fire and had no idea who did. Officer Ross interrupted him by saying, "See here, my boy, you forget that little window which looks into the space back of the organ from the other room. You needn't try to tell any foolish stories to me, for you were seen from the moment you came on the stage until you left after starting the fire."

Earl broke down and confessed, and as there was a witness to the questioning in the room, there was nothing Earl could do but repeat his confession to his parents and college authorities.

The *Ypsilanti Commercial* of Thursday, January 4, 1900, reported:

> *Earl stated that he had heaped a pile of papers about the rear of the organ and had set fire to them with matches. He planned the deed of mischief while he was in the chapel reading dime novels to Bell and Robtoy and on the way down stairs had made the excuse of going back to look for his gloves. When he left the two boys he hurried to the organ, gathered up loose papers, set fire to them and then in haste rejoined his companions with the gloves in his hand. He states positively that Bell and Robtoy were neither of them in any way concerned in the deed and that they did not even then know how and by whom the fire was started.*

When asked why he had set the fire, Earl at first said he did not know but then admitted it was in a fit of anger at the authorities of the Normal for attaching an electric motor to the bellows of the organ and depriving him of his position of blow boy. "Earl has the dime novel craze and is described as a willful, ungovernable boy," noted the *Ypsilanti Commercial*.

Earl was sent to the reform school at Lansing for three years. For putting out the fire, Rex Buell was given free use of the organ for as long as he remained at the Normal as well as free instruction. The old main building of the Normal was demolished in 1948. The organ was sold, the pipes were used to restore other organs and the wood was used to make furniture.

The Mysterious Death of William Benz

William and Lydia Benz seemed to be the perfect couple in the summer of 1903 with a bright and happy future before them. Married about nine months, each was devoted to the other. They lived happily on their farm about two or three miles south of the village of Dexter, in Lima Township. William had purchased the farm from a Mr. Yeager, and it included 145 acres, nineteen head of cattle, five horses, seventy-five sheep and a lot of farming utensils. The Benzes' happiness came to an end on Friday, August 21, 1903. That morning, Lydia hinted that she wanted to visit her father, William Aprill, in Scio Township.

"Go ahead," said William. "Take the horse. I'll not need him today and I can get my own dinner. Don't worry about me."

He went to hitch the horse, and she left his dinner on the table, consisting of four slices of bread, two slices of cake, butter, honey and a pitcher of milk. She forgot to put spoons on the table. Her husband always ate his bread and milk with a big spoon, but he knew where the spoons were kept. Lydia set off at 9:30 a.m.

She returned home that evening between 7:30 and 8:00 p.m. As she came to the farm, she noticed the cattle were still in the field. She stopped her horse and opened the gate, and the cattle followed her home. When she

The farm of William Aprill, the father-in-law of William Benz, as it appeared in the *Portrait and Biographical Album of Washtenaw County*, published in 1891. It was here Lydia went to visit on the day her husband died. *Used with permission of the Ypsilanti Historical Society.*

arrived at the house, she unhitched the horse, put him out and went to the house. She was surprised that William was not there to greet her.

At the back door she noticed blood and wondered if William had hurt himself. The kitchen door was unlocked. She found more blood in the kitchen and considerably more in the dining room. By now alarmed, she screamed, called her husband's name and looked around for him. Not finding him, she ran out of the house to go to a neighbor's.

On the road she met a boy named Hugh Quinn. With Quinn, she went to the home of Louis Traub. The three went back to the Benz house and searched for William. They followed a trail of blood from the dining room through the kitchen and across the yard to a shed. There, at the rear end of the building, they found the body of William, his throat cut from ear to ear. His face was covered with blood and was almost unrecognizable. The body was in a sitting position and rested on the top of a barrel, the left arm hanging down over the edge so the body had not fallen to the ground. On the ground near the body was a straight razor covered with blood.

The Washtenaw County coroner, Benjamin F. Watts, and Dr. R.B. Honey of Dexter were at once summoned to the farm. Dr. Honey arrived at the farm between 10:00 and 11:00 p.m. He saw the body of Benz still held up by the barrel in the shed. Coroner Watts may have arrived at about the same time and also saw the body in the shed. At first, Watts was inclined to accept the theory of suicide.

The body was carried to the kitchen, where the face was washed. Then Watts and Honey saw two holes in the right front of the skull that could have been made by the claws of a hammer. There was a bruise on the right cheek and another on the upper lip that appeared to have been made by a blow from a blunt instrument. These observations, and the fact that the body was found some seventy-five yards from the dining room and its bloodstained floor, proved that it would have been impossible for a man with his throat cut to walk that distance, causing Coroner Watts and Dr. Honey to consider the possibility of murder.

William Aprill, the father of Lydia, had arrived at the farm after Coroner Watts and Dr. Honey. He swept away the big pool of blood by the dining room door before the body was carried into the house so that blood would not be tracked into the house. He noticed there were no bloody footprints.

Washtenaw County Sheriff Joseph Gauntlett was informed of the death on Saturday, and he and Deputy Sheriff Peterson went to the house that day to carry out an investigation. That same day, Mrs. Benz found in the kitchen two cups and four spoons, with a little coffee in each of the cups. Later, she would say there was no milk in the cups, and William always had milk with his coffee. On the dining room floor was found a heavy hammer. Mrs. Benz had left the hammer on the table the morning before, as William had planned to pound nails into a fence that day. She also found a piece of paper on the floor, on which was written, "One white table cloth." The handwriting was neither that of William or of Mrs. Benz.

The sheath to the razor was found under the dining room table as well. The razor was kept in a drawer in a cupboard in the kitchen near the outer door. On the wall near the drawer was a bloody handprint, which only could have been made by someone reaching into the house from outside. The handprint was washed away before it could be compared to the hand of William Benz.

On the morning of his death, it was learned that William Benz had engaged Louis Traub and Hugh Quinn to haul oats on Saturday. He then returned to the house, put the horse in the shed and ate his dinner. After putting the horse in the shed, Benz had not removed the harness from the horse, which meant that he planned to resume work after dinner.

An hour after Benz would have finished his dinner, a neighbor saw a man crossing the yard behind the house. The neighbor thought nothing of this, as the neighbor was some distance away and he assumed it was Benz.

It was noted that there was a lot of blood in the kitchen and dining room but little blood on the path to the shed. There was no blood in the shed on the path from the door to where the body was found but plenty of blood on a wheelbarrow and a barrel that was on its side. The body might have been carried sideways over the wheelbarrow and barrel, as Benz could not have walked over these objects. The wheelbarrow and barrel were found in the way of the door to the shed, and it would have been impossible for Benz, as he was dying, to have stepped over these.

Drops of blood were found on a pump some six to eight feet off the path of blood, appearing as if someone had washed the blood from his hands.

Coroner Watts, in order to make certain of all the facts, ordered a postmortem to be carried out the following Monday. Dr. Theo Klingmann, an authority on surgery, was selected for the work. Dr. Klingmann, accompanied by Dr. Honey and Coroner Watts, went to the Benz home on Monday morning to examine the body. Dr. Klingmann later gave the *Washtenaw Evening Times* a statement regarding the wounds he found on the body of William Benz.

1. *Right forehead. A severe blow. Cut one-half inch in length. Bone not crushed.*
2. *Right jaw. Bruise but no cut.*
3. *Right cheek. Skin cut quite deeply for an inch in length. Discoloration one inch in diameter.*
4. *Fracture behind ear and at base of the brain caused by a blow delivered in front of and a little below the right ear. This blow was the most severe and caused a discoloration for two inches in diameter behind the ear. Bone of broken skull extended inwards.*
5. *Chest. Contusion three inches in diameter at point about at the breast bone.*
6. *Throat. Cut nearly from ear to ear. Went to the bone and severed the wind-pipe*

Dr. Klingmann was asked if a man could receive a blow on the back of the head, as indicated, and still retain consciousness. "Not probable. It is possible, but not at all likely," answered Dr. Klingmann.

"Could a man receive all the blows indicated and not be knocked down?"

"No."

"In your opinion, was it murder or suicide?"

"I do not desire to express an opinion as to that, but it hardly seems possible that a man could inflict upon himself all the wounds which I found on the body of Mr. Benz. But I want to think it over."

The investigation into the death of Benz continued through the weekend. Detective Peterson was asked his opinion of the case. "It is unquestionably suicide. I think my record as an officer is such that when a crime has been committed I will follow up any clue that may lead to the criminal and will go as far as anybody. But in this case the crime of murder was not committed."

"Have you figured out the circumstances and how it was done?"

He answered:

> *Judging from the surroundings, I should say Benz was in the yard and under an uncontrollable impulse; he attacked himself with the hammer, intending to kill himself. He struck himself on the forehead and then sat down upon a chicken coop. Half crazed by the blows, he struck himself again and again in a wild manner. He then went into the house and got his razor from the cupboard and these little spatterings came from nobody but Benz and the blood spattered from his head as he was reaching up to the top shelf for the razor. There is also blood from finger marks on the cupboard door. Benz then went into the dining room and cut his throat with the razor. He then went out to the woodshed and expired. Whether or not the final cut was made in the house or in the woodshed I do not know, but he certainly used the razor on himself in the house. There are three slashes in the throat.*

Washtenaw County Sheriff Gauntlett was of the same opinion:

> *There is not a sign of a struggle anywhere. The body was not dragged and, what is more, I am positive that Benz was not attacked in the house. If somebody had knocked him down with the hammer he would have fallen upon his own blood. Either an arm, leg, hand or the body would have touched some drop of blood and spread it out, but every drop is clear and the spatterings such as would come from naturally fallen from the wounds and while he was standing up with his head bent forward. The*

blood leading from the rooms to the woodshed have every appearance that he was staggering headlong to the woodshed. The spatterings are forward in direction.

One reason given against the suicide theory was that Benz was not pressed for money, yet Sheriff Gauntlett and Detective Peterson had found someone who said otherwise. In the spring, Benz had been riding with a hired hand, Chris Kuhn. The two had a pint of whiskey and a gallon of beer.

"Ain't you going pretty heavily into debt for this farm?" asked Kuhn.

"Yes," replied Benz. "But if worse comes to worst, I can go jump in the river, or do this," making a motion with his hand as if cutting his own throat.

As soon as the body was discovered, suspicion fell on a man named Fred Jaeger, who had been employed by Benz until he was fired on July 21. Jaeger and a man named Van Fleet had stopped by the Benz farm on the Tuesday before Benz died to collect some personal belongings. Investigators learned that on the day of Benz's death, Jaeger and Van Fleet had entered Nissie's stable in Manchester at noon and put out their horse. They returned at 5:00 p.m. and tried to sell the horse. Failing to do so, they sent word to relatives to come and get the horse. Then the two had hired on with a small circus that was in Hillsdale. This is where Sheriff Gauntlett found them and called them to one side.

"Do you know where William Benz is?" asked the sheriff.

"He must be in Dexter," answered Jaeger. "I saw him there Tuesday."

"No," said Sheriff Gauntlett. "Benz is dead."

The news clearly impressed Jaeger. Jaeger and Van Fleet returned to Ann Arbor with Sheriff Gauntlett as witnesses to testify at the inquest.

The family of Mrs. Benz had commissioned former Sheriff Michael Brennan to ascertain where Jaeger was on the day of the death. "I found," said Brennan, "that he was in Manchester at 11 o'clock and was there the remainder of the day. He certainly had nothing to do with the case."

No account of the case explains why Jaeger was fired from the employ of Benz or why suspicion fell on him so quickly.

The funeral of William Benz was held on the morning of Tuesday, August 25, 1903, at the Salem Lutheran Church in Scio Township. The church, although a large building, could not contain all the relatives and friends who had come to pay their last respects. The pastor, Reverend Kaarer, preached an effective sermon. The rules of the German Lutheran Church were severe: the body of a suicide could not be brought into the church. But as the majority of farmers were of the opinion that Benz had been murdered, there was no objection to his receiving a Christian burial. After the service, however, the trustees of the cemetery had the body placed in a vault instead of in the ground.

This came as no surprise to those familiar with how the cemetery had been managed since it was founded. There were no family lots; each body was buried in turn as it was brought in. Families were broken up, with each grave of a family member set some distance apart, depending on how much time had passed between each death. This suited the convenience of the trustees who, when one section of ground was filled, laid out another one. The one exception to this rule was married couples, who could purchase two lots so they could be buried side by side.

Lydia Benz attended the funeral of her husband with Dr. Klingmann nearby in case she should collapse. Since the discovery of the body of William, she had been in a state of almost total collapse. At times, she would drop off in a fainting spell, and at others she would burst out weeping. She was being cared for by members of her family.

The inquest into the death of William Benz was held on Thursday, August 27, 1903, in the Opera House at Dexter, the only building large enough in the village to hold the crowd of six to seven hundred who wished to hear the testimony. Among those present were Prosecuting Attorney Duffy and Attorney John F. Lawrence, retained by William Aprill. Coroner Watts presided impressively as testimony was taken down by a stenographer.

The first witness called was Lydia Benz, who told of leaving her husband to visit her father and returning home to find the body. She said their marriage was a happy one and they were not troubled by debt. William had purchased the farm from Mr. Yeager for $8,000. They had a mortgage for $4,000, payable in seven years with a 4 percent interest. The mortgage had been reduced to $1,900. No interest was due until the following March.

She said she thought there was about a quart of blood in the dining room. On a table, she indicated a space of ten inches in diameter, which she said was covered with blood about a half inch thick. A little blood was found on the back porch, and only a few drops were found on the stoop to the shed. Blood had spurted to the ceiling of the dining room and fallen in pools on the floor.

Hugh Quinn and Louis Traub were sworn in, and each testified to the finding of the body and that William Benz had talked to each of them on the morning of the day he died about hauling oats the next Saturday. Quinn said he had worked for Benz for several months and had lived with the family and taken his meals with them. He said the relationship between William and Lydia Benz had always been pleasant.

The next witness called was Dr. Theo Klingmann, who described the wounds he had found on the body during the postmortem. Dr. Klingmann said the blood must have come from the wounds in the throat. Further, he said, Benz was alive when the body reached the shed. The skin, he said, had been cut at least twice. He was of the opinion that the throat had been cut once in the dining room and again in the shed.

Coroner Watts asked Dr. Klingmann, "In your opinion, could a man, with his throat cut as you found him, possibly walk from the sitting room to the woodshed?"

Dr. Klingmann answered, "No."

Dr. Honey was called as a witness after dinner and talked of seeing the body in the shed and of the wounds found on the body by Dr. Klingmann during the postmortem. He said there was a big pool of blood to the right of the dining room table, on the other side of the table and scattered drops of blood leading into the kitchen. A blow on the breastbone had left a mark the size of a quarter dollar when he first saw it on Friday night, but on Monday during the postmortem it was larger than a silver dollar.

Sheriff Gauntlett described the bloodstains as he saw them on Saturday morning between 10:00 and 11:00 a.m. "The drops of blood leading from the dining room through the kitchen all spattered equally in all directions from which he deduced the conclusion that they fell perpendicular, but the drops of blood on the porch and path spattered forward from which he deduced that at this point they had spurted forward. There were no bloody footprints. He looked careful for them," reported the *Ypsilanti Sentinel-Commercial* of September 3, 1903.

Deputy Peterson testified as to his conclusions that Benz had killed himself but could give no reason why Benz should commit suicide. He said there were bloody marks made by a bloody hand in opening the cupboard door where the razor was kept and blood spots inside the cupboard. He said there were no bloody footprints.

The jury returned with a verdict: "William E. Benz came to his death on the 21st of August, 1903, between the hours of 10 o'clock a. m. and 7:30 p.m. on his farm in the township of Lima by having his throat cut by a person or persons unknown to the jury."

After the inquest, Prosecutor Duffy said, "If anybody can furnish any clue I will prosecute the case. I am ready to do business." No clue was ever furnished, and no one was prosecuted.

"Now that the jury has stated practically that it was murder," noted the *Washtenaw Daily Times* of Friday, August 28, 1903, "the body will be given regular burial in the Lutheran churchyard." In this, the *Times* was mistaken.

William Aprill, the father-in-law, made arrangements for a lot in the German cemetery in Dexter, and these arrangements were accepted. Then, when the grave was dug and the body ready for interment, cemetery authorities ordered a halt. They were still not convinced that the death was not due to suicide. As the death might be due to suicide, the authorities of the cemetery would not permit the burial of the body, in accordance with the rules of their faith. William Benz, the father, had a lot in the cemetery in Dexter, and, because of the trouble over the lot Aprill had arranged for, he ordered his son buried in his lot, which he had control over.

Lydia Benz never remarried, and she returned to the home of her father. Later she moved to Ann Arbor, where, for a time, Harold Benz, the younger brother of William who in 1920 was fifteen years of age, stayed with her. She continued to live in Ann Arbor into the 1940s. Every year, the Ann Arbor city directories listed her as the widow of William.

Rise and Fall of Frank P. Glazier

F rank P. Glazier of Chelsea rose to the pinnacle of political success in the state of Michigan only to fall to the very bottom of failure. When at the top, he held the office of treasurer of the state of Michigan, with his eyes fixed on the office of governor. Instead of holding the governor's office, Glazier would occupy a prison cell.

Frank Porter Glazier was born in Jackson, Michigan, on March 8, 1862, the son of George Pickering Glazier and Emily J. (Stimson) Glazer. The family moved to Chelsea, where Frank attended the public schools. He continued his education at Michigan State University, graduating in 1880 from the pharmaceutical department. He completed a course at the Eastman National Business College of Poughkeepsie, New York, graduating with the class of 1881. Glazier married Henrietta Geddes of Chelsea on December 30, 1880. The couple traveled in Germany for six months, visiting many points of historic, modern and scenic interest.

When the couple returned to Chelsea in November, Glazier purchased the drugstore of his father and continued the successful enterprise until 1890, when he sold the business. That year, Glazier turned his interest to the manufacture of oil stoves. The Glazier Strong Stove Company made three-burner kerosene stoves for cooking and heating. After two years, he purchased the interests of the others in the business. In 1901, the business was incorporated under the name of the Glazier Stove Company with Frank

Frank P. Glazier as state treasurer. *Used with permission of the Bentley Historical Library, University of Michigan.*

as president and general manager. The company employed some 150 to 200 and claimed to produce the "brightest and best" oil and gas stoves that were sold throughout the country.

In 1901, Glazier erected a fine stone and marble building at 122 South Main Street for the Chelsea Savings Bank at a cost of $100,000 as a memorial to his father, who had died that year. Glazier was elected president of the bank in 1902 and had previously served for a number of years as a director.

At about this time, Glazier had a new office building constructed for the stove works that would include the tall water and clock tower that is still a landmark of Chelsea today.

Past and Present of Washtenaw County by Samuel Beakes, published in 1906, noted:

Mr. Glazier is a Republican, politically prominent and has become widely known through the state by reason of his active and effective support of the party. He was president of the village for five years in 1898 and again from 1901 to 1904, inclusive. During this time many substantial and important improvements were instituted. He stood as the champion of all that was progressive and his labors contributed in huge measure to the advancement of the town. Still higher political honors awaited him; however, for in 1902 he was elected to the state senate and was there connected with important constructive legislation, being an active worker in committee rooms. In 1904 he was elected state treasurer, being nominated by acclamation at the state convention, an honor not given to any candidate on his first term in thirty years.

In 1906, Glazier went about constructing the tallest building then in Ann Arbor when he purchased land at the corner of Main and Huron in what was then the biggest real estate transaction in the history of Ann Arbor. This was to have been named the Glazier Building, but by the time it was completed in 1908, Glazier was no longer the owner. The building would be named the First National Building and renamed after that bank moved to its own structure.

"During the years from 1904 to 1907 Mr. Glazier was easily one of the three most prominent political figures in the state," reported the *Ann Arbor News*. "It was an open secret that he coveted the governorship of Michigan, and one of his moves to this end was the founding of a daily newspaper here, *The Ann Arbor News*."

Glazier was at the top of his career, and now he began to fall. As the treasurer, he deposited state funds in banks throughout the state, including his bank at Chelsea. As the Michigan State Supreme Court reported:

During his entire term of office as State treasurer, from January 1, 1905, till January 30, 1908, when he resigned, respondent was president, director, principal stockholder, chairman of the discount committee, and active manager of the Chelsea Savings Bank of Chelsea, a village of some 2,000 inhabitants. The capital stock of the bank was increased from $60,000 to $100,000 on December 28, 1905. For many years prior to 1905 the bank had been a State depository of public funds. Soon after January 1, 1905, and again soon after January 1, 1907, respondent *entered into contracts with the bank, signed by himself as State treasurer, on the one hand, and as president of the bank, on the other hand, providing for the deposit of State money in said bank.*

As president of the bank, Glazier unlawfully appropriated at different times, to his own use, different sums belonging to the state and in his custody as state treasurer. Glazier had used his position as president of the bank and as president of the Stove Company to secure loans from a number of banks. When the banks that had made the loans to Glazier called in the loans, Glazier was unable to pay up. As it turned out, Glazier was in debt for some $1,078,000 to eight banks, and his debt was backed by the Stove Company, which could not cover the debt.

Louis Wm. Doll asked in his book, *Less Than Immortal: The Rise and Fall of Frank Porter Glazier of Chelsea, Michigan*:

> *How did it happen that such a large amount of money was advanced by any bank without knowing what the other banks were doing? They simply never asked, and he never volunteered the information. A possible*

Chelsea as it appeared in the early twentieth century, with the Glazier Stove Works in the background and the clock tower, which were built by Glazier. *Used with permission of the Bentley Historical Library, University of Michigan. From the Sam Sturgis collection, Box #5.*

Glazier wanted to hold the office of governor but instead ended up in Jackson Prison. *From Michigan Manual, 1913.*

explanation is that he was Frank P. Glazier, wealthy manufacturer, state treasurer with the power of depositing or withholding state funds from banks, and possible future governor of the state, and they did not want to offend him. It was very unbusiness like and left Glazier badly extended in any case. It was true that the bank loans were secured by Stove Company stock, but with the company in receivership, what would the stock be worth as security?

In the end, Glazier resigned as state treasurer, stood trial and was convicted. He was sentenced to serve not less than five years and not more than ten years. He was pardoned after two years and spent the rest of his life at his home on Cavanaugh Lake, where he died on the evening of January 1, 1922.

A street in northeast Ann Arbor was named for Frank Glazier but has often been changed by city sign makers to "Glacier Way"; it is once again labeled as "Glazier Way." The bank building he constructed as a memorial to his father is now the Fourteenth District Courthouse.

Scio Night Raiders

D r. Neil Gates of 117 East Liberty, Ann Arbor, was accustomed to calls and traveling to care for those who were ill. He was called out on Sunday, November 9, 1907, to Lodi Township, east of Ann Arbor, for that very reason. Once he had finished the call, he began the trip back to Ann Arbor in his automobile. As he was driving through Scio Township, his car ran out of gas. He also found himself stuck in the mud. Dr. Gates walked to the home of George Schnierie, who gave Dr. Gates a ride back into Ann Arbor.

Dr. Gates was busy all day Monday so was unable to recover his automobile until the afternoon of Tuesday, November 12. A Mr. Koch, of Koch's repair shop, went with him to help bring the vehicle back. When they arrived at the place where the automobile was parked, they found it a burnt-out wreck. Someone had piled hay and grass around the vehicle and set it on fire. The body of the car was badly damaged, and the engine was ruined. An expensive lap robe that Dr. Gates had left in the car was missing. Beside the car was a bottle of whiskey.

The car was taken to Koch's repair shop, but only the metal parts could be saved. It cost Dr. Gates over $500 to have the car repaired. The township officers were informed of the act, and Dr. Gates offered a $50 reward for anyone who could provide information leading to the arrest and conviction of the offenders. The reward would go unclaimed until the following July.

In July 1908, two young men were caught destroying a hayrack belonging to Christian Heft, who secured a warrant for them. Then John Springman had a warrant issued for Jack Hartman, Henry Klager and Louis Schwartz on a charge of destroying a newly erected wire fence by cutting the stays.

Deputy Sheriff Stark had long suspected Klager of having played a part in the burning of Dr. Gates's car but never had evidence to support the belief. When he invited Klager to "come along," Stark said to Klager: "You'd better bring that blanket of Dr. Gates along with you, you know the other boys have given away that deal and they lay it all to you."

Klager at first denied involvement in the burning of the car, but in the end he admitted his part. He told Stark the blanket was buried in a field behind the house, and the two spent some time searching for it, without success. Klager was taken to Ann Arbor and placed in the jail there. The others soon confessed their roles in the burning of the car.

Klager admitted that he and his friends were a little intoxicated when they came across the car of Dr. Gates. They tried all the levers on the car but were unable to make it run. Deciding the car was no good anyway, Klager said they emptied the gasoline from the tank over the car.

This was the beginning of the end of a feud that had lasted twenty years.

Back in the 1840s, John Springman and Joseph Wagner were the heads of two German households who had crossed the ocean and settled in Scio Township. They chose as their homes adjoining farms and for forty years were good neighbors and warm friends. Each helped the other, visited and drank each other's cider. They prospered and were considered wealthy, as wealth was counted in that rural district. But because of a pig, it began to change.

In about 1888, a pig belonging to Wagner began to crawl under the line fence marking the boundary of their property and causing mischief on Springman's land. This maliciously inclined pig died suddenly, and Wagner went around saying that Springman had something to do with the death of the pig. Springman sued Wagner for slander and won the case. For the next twenty years, Springman said, the Wagners got even at every opportunity.

Although there were now bad feelings between the families, things did not become serious during the life of Joseph Wagner. During these years, Rudolph, Joe's son, was growing into a big strapping lad, and early in life, he engendered the animus of Springman by raiding his orchard and melon patch.

Joseph Wagner died in 1903, and Rudolph proceeded to take charge of the 166-acre farm. In addition, he inherited a sense of malice toward Springman. Joe Wagner was, as Springman said, hardly "under the sod" when Springman began to suffer from night depredations. For the next four years, Springman and his friends were the victims of a steady run of malicious acts.

For the most part, the acts were considered petty, as a garden was uprooted, the strands of a wire fence were clipped or stock were set free by way of an open gate so that Springman had to chase them in the morning for miles. Not all of the acts were considered petty, however.

On one occasion a load of hay belonging to Springman that was left on a hilltop was set rolling down the steep incline, scattering the load and overturning and demolishing the wagon. The night raiders pulled the posts of a line fence, and over three hundred feet of the fence were leveled. Not only that, but the wire was also cut in a way as to make the fence worthless. In the fall of 1907, several acres of shocked corn on the Springman farm were scattered. Springman found shocks placed in trees and on the barn; bands were cut and the fodder scattered.

The *Ypsilanti Daily Press* noted:

> *It was a common thing for Springman to find his wagons and buggies mounted on the barn or on the straw stacks of a morning. It was nothing out of the ordinary for him to find a portion of his corn field or a field grain leveled by ruthless trampling. A corn harvester was taken to pieces, the bolts and burrs scattered and the machine rendered worthless. On more than one occasion Springman visited his barn in the morning to find his cattle tied and harnessed in ridiculous position in their stalls.*

One night the night raiders entered Springman's barn and led his horse out of its stall and onto the floor. Hay ropes were tied to the horse's feet and tail, and the animal was lifted bodily from the floor and into the air. The feet of the horse were tied together, and the horse was left to suffer. In the morning, Springman entered the barn, found the horse and cut it down. The horse was never able to stand again, and within a week it died.

Springman was not the only victim of the night raiders. On another occasion, they removed all the nuts and bolts from a corn binder belonging to Ben Scheilman and Robert Jedele and left the nuts and bolts piled in a heap.

Springman and others became desperate over the persecution being carried out on them and began to keep watch at night. Once the first five raiders were identified and warrants were issued, Deputy Sheriff Stark invited them in for a talk at the county jail. They, in turn, named the others involved.

The total list of those involved was: Joe Beam, age thirty, Louis Beam, thirty-one, and Otto Beam, seventeen, all brothers; Jacob Hartman, twenty-one, and George Hartman, nineteen, also brothers; Rudolph Wagner, twenty-four; Henry Klager, twenty-seven; Louis Schwartz, twenty; Louis Weidman, twenty-one; Henry Weidman, twenty-four; and John Burkhardt, twenty-two.

Once the night raiders were rounded up by Deputy Sheriff Stark, it became clear that young Wagner was the leader. The *Ypsilanti Daily Press* noted:

> *Tall and angular, his black curly hair topping sharp eyes and a square jaw, he is the picture of a strong man. When the band was questioned in the Washtenaw county jail on each occasion they seemed by instinct to wait for Wagner to speak first. Wagner himself never confessed guilt to any of the depredations until the statements of his mates so bound him that further denial was useless. Then he stolidly admitted each point in the story.*

When questioned about the burning of Dr. Gates's car, Wagner denied that they intended to set it on fire. "We went there with some juice and thought to fill it and run it away," said Wagner. "Gasoline was spilled, someone scratched a match and the thing caught fire. We fought it all we could but we couldn't save it. No, we weren't scared, but we did bury the blanket in the field."

On the afternoon of July 14, 1908, nine of the young men found themselves standing before Justice Gibson. Four of them—Rudolph Wagner, John Burkhardt, Henry Weidman and Louis Schwartz—were charged with cruelty to animals, Springman's horse, and were fined twenty-five and costs each. Then Henry Klager, Louis Schwartz and Jacob Hartman were fined ten dollars and costs each for destroying the fence of Springman.

Justice Gibson delivered a severe lecture to the young men, telling them that if any of them ever appeared before him again on any charge, he would not let them off so easily but would give them the limit of the law.

Then six of them—Joe Beam, Henry Klager, Rudolph Wagner, Louis Weidman, Louis Schwartz and John Burkhardt—were bound over to the circuit court on the charge of burning the car of Dr. Gates. The six were released upon furnishing a bond of $300 each. Justice Gibson advised the young men to make restitution so they could appear before the circuit court with as clean a record as possible.

Deputy Sheriff Stark collected the reward of fifty dollars offered by Dr. Gates.

Springman filed a lawsuit against those who had tormented him for so long. The cases appear to have been settled quickly and quietly out of court.

Lodi Township Shooting

W hat is perhaps one of the most mysterious shootings to have occurred in Washtenaw County happened in the township of Lodi, which is to the south and west of Ann Arbor, on the night of Sunday, May 2, 1909, when Jacob Lombard, a nineteen-year-old farm lad, accidentally shot himself. That Lombard shot himself is not the mystery, and that it was an accident was never in question. The mystery is the circumstances by which he came to shoot himself.

Lombard was the son of Mary Lombard, a widow whose husband had died not long before. The estate was in the process of being settled when the shooting occurred. The family was said to have been immensely wealthy. Even so, young Lombard was employed by his uncle on a farm near Saline, and his sisters were employed in homes in Ann Arbor. Lombard and his sisters visited their mother on Sunday, May 2, 1903, to attend a confirmation in the Scio Church.

That evening, young Lombard gave his sisters a ride in a carriage to where they could take the interurban back to Ann Arbor. The trip was made without incident, and once the sisters were off, Lombard began the trip back to where his mother lived. He would make this trip alone. The carriage was pulled by a horse described as being young and fractious. This much is known for sure. The mystery is what happened next.

Late that evening, very late, Lombard returned to the house in a state of semi-collapse. He was wet and covered in mud. To explain, Lombard told his mother that he had been set upon by two masked men in a dark spot about a mile from the house. The men, said Lombard, pulled the horse up short and then seized Lombard and pulled him from the carriage.

"The pair wasted few words," reported the *Ypsilanti Daily Press* of Monday, May 3, 1909, "as though they feared their voices would reveal their identity, and began to beat Lombard unmercifully. After pounding him until they were tired they threw him down and dragged him by the heels through a nearby pond of stagnant water and mud. Then they walked away, leaving Lombard to return home the best he could."

He told his mother he was going back to get the horse and asked for a rusty old revolver that had belonged to his father to take as protection. Securing the revolver, he was looking it over as he stepped out of the house. His mother followed him out of the house as he did. She stood in the door and watched as he fiddled with the revolver.

This was an old-fashioned weapon, and it was necessary to hold back the trigger while the chamber was swung into place. As Lombard was attempting to swing the one cartridge into place, the trigger let fly, and the bullet was discharged while the muzzle of the revolver was pointed directly at the face of Lombard. The bullet passed through his nose and into his brain. Young Lombard was dead in minutes.

"A pathetic feature of the affair," noted the *Daily Times News* of Monday, May 3, 1909, "is the fact that the mother was alone a time and although neighbors were summoned and reached there before the officers, the body still remained in the yard where it had fallen until their arrival."

The officers arrived as soon as possible and spent the rest of the night and early morning tracking Lombard's movements of the night before. They soon reached the conclusion that Lombard had made up the story of being attacked by two men. The horse, they reasoned, had been frightened by a dog that had run out at the horse. The horse, frightened, ran away, pulling the carriage behind it.

The *Daily Times News* reported:

> The tracks, which were followed for several miles, show where the horse
> started to run with the driver attempting to hang on and directing him for a
> space. Later the animal broke away from the carriage and still the plucky

boy hung on to the reins. The tracks further show where he was dragged through the mud and mire and where he attempted to turn the frightened animal into the fence but without success.

There was no evidence on the body of a beating, but the cuts and bruises on Lombard's body appeared as if made by being dragged, as at the end of the reins. Supporting this theory was the fact that the horse had run away with Lombard at the reins before. Because of this, Lombard had been reproved several times at home. When Lombard arrived at home that night, the officers suspected, he told the story of the beating to keep from being reproved again. The story gave him an excuse to go back for the horse and a reason to ask for the gun, which he most likely intended to use on the dog.

Everyone agreed that the shooting was an accident, and the coroner decided an inquest was not needed. The three sisters whom Lombard had driven to the interurban station returned on Monday to attend his funeral. The funeral was held at the house on Wednesday morning of that week, with services at Scio Church.

Body in the Barn

Mrs. Mary Nordham of West Middle Street in the village of Chelsea went to the door of her neighbor, Mrs. Elizabeth Stapish, who was then seventy-three years of age, on the morning of Thursday, September 25, 1913, to buy some potatoes. Mrs. Stapish had a garden and sold produce. Mrs. Nordham rapped on the door and received no response; she went away for a time and returned that afternoon. Once again, she rapped on the door but received no response. This time, she noticed that the doors to the house were unlocked. Mrs. Nordham knew Mrs. Stapish never left her home without locking the doors.

Elizabeth Stapish was born Elizabeth Schwickerath in 1842 in the province of Lorraine, Germany. At the age of twenty-seven, she crossed the Atlantic Ocean to settle in the village of Chelsea. She married John Stapish, and the two lived in the house on West Middle Street until his death in 1901.

Neighbors searched the house at about 4:00 p.m., thinking she may have fallen ill. Mrs. Stapish had been seen for the past few days walking back and forth between her house and barn, where she had been husking corn. In the house, they found a package of meat on the table, still wrapped in the paper provided by the store. The meat had turned putrid. Mrs. Stapish's pocketbook was on the table beside the meat. The walking skirt and cape that she wore when she went out were found hanging on a nail. Her hat was in its usual place. A search of the house failed to turn up any trace of Mrs. Stapish.

Now the neighbors gathered to talk over the situation among themselves. Mrs. Stapish was always considered mildly deluded and was known to hold some peculiar notions, and she attracted particular attention because of her fondness for colors in her attire. She was known for her peacock green dress and liked to wear petticoats of yellow and red. She was also noticed because of her headdress of many hues. Mrs. Stapish, it was known, had once been an inmate in an insane asylum. The neighbors wondered if she had killed herself, but none had noticed any indications of despondency or had heard her say anything to lead anyone to think she was contemplating suicide. One of the neighbors, a Mr. Brooks, called Deputy Sheriff J. Edward McKune, who hurried to the house and began a systematic search of the house and the outbuildings.

At about 5:30 p.m., Deputy Sheriff McKune made a search of the barn behind the house. This is where Mrs. Stapish had been seen husking corn. The barn was a one-story building with two windows and one door. The windows were covered with dust and did not appear to have been opened in years. The door, Deputy Sheriff McKune found, was latched on the outside. Inside the barn, in the center of the floor, Deputy Sheriff McKune found a pile of cornstalks in the shape of a human form. Brushing aside the cornstalks, McKune found the body of Mrs. Stapish.

She was lying on her back with her hands on her chest. The face of Mrs. Stapish was terribly discolored, as she had died of strangulation. Her tongue and eyes were protruding. A strap, such as that used on a trunk or suitcase, was tied around her neck and was so tightly drawn that it was imbedded in the flesh. The buckle of the belt was at the back of her neck. The strap was drawn through the ring but was not buckled. Her legs were bound with a sisal cord, such as that used to tie corn. The head was covered by a few sheets of a newspaper drenched with blood. On the head were a number of abrasions and other disfigurements near both the right and left temples. Bits of material from the silo might have been used as a gag, as there was suspicion of an "unspeakable" crime—rape—preceding the death.

Deputy Sheriff McKune at once informed Sheriff Stark and Prosecuting Attorney Burke at Ann Arbor. The two hurried to Chelsea in an automobile. Before they arrived, Justice of the Peace Herbert D. Witherell, who was acting as the coroner, gave permission to remove the body to Staffan's undertaking parlor on Main Street. This was done to expedite the investigation and the holding of the inquest. Nothing around the body was moved. As soon as Prosecuting Attorney Burke and Sheriff Stark arrived, they searched every nook and corner of the barn for possible clues. George Grant, the Washtenaw County clerk, who lived in Chelsea, went over the grounds of the house with a searchlight in the hope of finding footprints.

One of the first things Prosecuting Attorney Burke did on arrival at Chelsea was to send for Doctors S.G. Bush and Andrus Guide. "Gentlemen, I want you to make a complete examination," said Burke, "so we can clear this thing up. I want nothing left undone to shed every possible light on how this woman came to her death."

The physicians said that the abrasions on the head of Mrs. Stapish may have been there several days before her death or may have been caused by the death struggle. Burke wanted the examination to include an analysis of the contents of the stomach to make certain Mrs. Stapish had not taken any poison. This was not possible, the physicians pointed out, as the body had been saturated with embalming fluid, some of which would have entered the stomach. By the end of the examination, the physicians could not establish beyond a doubt whether the "unspeakable" crime had preceded the death. The doctors did determine that Mrs. Stapish had died of strangulation. The doctors said there was nothing about the body that precluded the possibility of her having committed suicide.

Those who suggested she had killed herself said she could have fastened a strap suspended from a rafter in the barn around her neck. Then, during the death struggle, she pulled down the cornstalks that covered her body.

There were a number of reasons to disagree with the theory of suicide, it was pointed out. "Mrs. Stapish, when she met her death, wore a large number of garments which one bent on suicide, would have shed. The fact that her legs were tied with sisal twine underneath the several skirts she had on, goes far toward offsetting the theory that she tied her lower limbs with her own hands," noted the *Daily Times News* of Friday, September 26, 1913. The article continued:

> *All of those who have had experience in ferreting out murder cases and who saw the body were agreed that the woman's legs were tied with the sole object of preventing her from kicking the fiend who assailed her or from possibly regaining her feet, after she had been knocked down by a blow that stunned her. Then she was strangled to make sure of her death. That is the plausible theory which is joined in by all who saw the body shortly after*

it was found and who unwilling in the face of these facts and the evidence that the hasp on the barn door was closed from the outside to let the matter rest by accepting the suicide theory.

Sheriff Stark and Deputies Sheriff Max and Eldert made a thorough search of the house and may have had something of a surprise. The house was one of the oldest in Chelsea and, on the outside, had a dilapidated appearance. Inside the house, they found hats in every color of the rainbow and in most gorgeous styles, a half dozen pairs of shoes, several of which had never been worn, rubbers and overshoes, blankets galore and an assortment of new silk underwear. There were all sorts of female wearing apparel, most of it more expensive than one would have expected from someone in the financial circumstances of Mrs. Stapish. The men may have been surprised to find that Mrs. Stapish, although she was childless, had purchased an assortment of baby bibs. These were only a few of the items the men found in the house.

The assortment of belongings found in the house was most likely a result of the mental illness Mrs. Stapish was afflicted with. She had been committed to the Pontiac insane asylum on May 10, 1888. At that time, Dr. F.A. Ackley had told the court she had been having insane spells for the previous ten years. She was moody and for some time would be silent and then suddenly jump up and say, "My husband is going to kill me." Her insanity, said Dr. Ackley, was a kind of melancholy. Dr. Thomas Shaw told the court she had no control over her faculties and he considered her not to be morally responsible. Her brother, Herbert Schwickerath, said she suffered from the delusion that her neighbors were in general unkind toward her. He said she was crazy on the subjects of religion and money. The doctors and her brother told the court that she would be a menace to the community if allowed to stay at large. She was sent to the Pontiac institution, from which she was released three years later.

When Mrs. Stapish was released from the asylum, she was considered incapable of handling her own affairs. Her brother was appointed her guardian and paid her an allowance from the small estate left her by her late husband. She earned some money by selling produce from her garden and the chickens she raised in her yard.

During the search of the house, Deputy Sheriff Matthew Max found a number of silver coins and some change wrapped in a piece of tissue paper and hidden in a salt bag. Sheriff Stark and his deputies began to wonder if maybe robbery was a motive for the murder of Mrs. Stapish after all. The search had failed to turn up any paper money, which was a surprise, as she seems to have hoarded everything that had come into her possession. She was believed to have had a number of hiding places for her money. Those who saw the inside of her house believed that she had a considerable sum of money hidden in the house, a belief based on the means she took to protect herself against theft. She had burglar alarms on the windows and doors and had devised a system of securing her trunks on wooden blocks so if anyone had tried to open or move one, there would have been a noise heard all through the house.

She may have returned from the butcher shop on Tuesday and, after changing her clothes, checked to see if anyone had tampered with her hiding places for her money. Someone may have observed Mrs. Stapish as she did and, coming upon her, struck a blow to the head. "Then tying her legs, the fiend might have finished the murderous deed by taking off his belt and strangling the woman with it…That the murderer would choose the method of making sure of his victim's death by strangling, is explained by the fact that he would believe it to be bloodless and therefore least liable to lead to his detection," noted the *Ann Arbor Daily Times News*. He then, it was suspected, tied her legs together to make it easier to carry her body to the barn. There he hid her under the cornstalks and locked the barn door from the outside to delay the discovery of the body. This was done, it was suggested, to give him time to get away.

From the beginning of the investigation, in their search for suspects, the sheriff and his deputies first looked to the end of Mrs. Stapish's backyard. Her yard backed to the Michigan Central Railroad tracks, and at the time of her death, there was a crew of about 150 men encamped in shacks behind her property. These men were employed in ballasting the tracks near Chelsea. They were in the habit of buying chickens and other produce from Mrs. Stapish. She tended to haggle over the price, and this may have led to the impression that she was a woman of considerable means. These men saw her come and go to and from the barn, and any one of them could have called to her. A few of these men chose not to buy chickens and produce from Mrs. Stapish but instead stole these items from her yard. There was a hole in the fence at the back of her property through which the men crawled to either buy her produce or steal her chickens. The sheriff and his deputies learned that the belt used to strangle Mrs. Stapish was the same kind used by the men working on the Michigan Central crew.

The coroner's jury met on Saturday, September 27, 1913, at first in the office of Justice of the Peace Witherell, who acted as coroner, and then later moved to the more spacious quarters of the town hall. At the inquest, Mary Nordham told of stopping by the house seeking Elizabeth Stapish and not finding her. She said the door to the barn where the body was found was locked from the outside. "She was very positive on this point," noted the *Chelsea Standard* of October 2, 1913, "but failed to remember that in opening the door it was necessary to lift it over a stone door rail."

The verdict of the jury was: "Mrs. Elizabeth Stapish came to her death by strangulation brought about by means of a leather strap about her neck in the hands of some person or persons unknown to the jury."

Sheriff Stark and his deputies, working on the theory that the death was caused by murder, traveled throughout southeast Michigan to question Michigan Central workers who were near the house at the time of Mrs. Stapish's death. After they questioned the last worker and were still unable to find a suspect, they moved on to other cases. In time, the death of Elizabeth Stapish faded from memory and is now all but forgotten.

Shooting of Attorney Mahon

An evening of innocent fun turned into near tragedy on Saturday, October 11, 1913, in Ypsilanti as a result of a joke. One man nearly died as another tried to be funny. They should have known better.

Edward Kennedy was a Detroit attorney who was a native of Ypsilanti and had graduated from the city school system. On October 11, 1913, Kennedy, his son Ted and daughter Faith started to motor to Ypsilanti to spend the weekend with his mother. They were still in downtown Detroit when they saw brothers Tom and Frank Mahon and asked if they would like to come along.

Frank Mahon was the clerk of the Wayne County Probate Court. Tom was forty years of age, and he had graduated from the University of Michigan Law School in 1896. He had been engaged in the practice of law in the city of Detroit since 1897. Although described as a prominent member of the Detroit bar, Tom Mahon may have been better known for a barroom brawl than for his legal skill.

The year before, on January 3, 1912, Tom Mahon and Attorney Edmond Joncas were standing in Louis Schneider's Saloon when they got into an argument with John F. Dodge, of the car company, and Robert E. Oakman, a real estate dealer. Oakman thought Mahon was going to attack him and knocked Mahon to the floor. Dodge took a punch at Mahon as well. Joncas got involved in the affair and was pummeled by Dodge. Bartenders broke up the fight.

Mahon believed he had grounds for a damage suit against Dodge and Oakman. Edward Kennedy represented Mahon in the negotiations with Dodge and Oakman, whereby Mahon received several thousand dollars from Oakman as part of the settlement and a considerable sum from Dodge. The case never went to court.

On that day in October 1913, Tom said that he had to be back in Detroit that evening but would run out with them and come back on the train. The party arrived at Ypsilanti at about 6:00 p.m. and had dinner at the Hawkins house. Then they went to the Michigan Central depot to see Tom off but found that the train was running a little late. The party stayed around downtown Ypsilanti, playing boyish pranks on friends. Their friends knew them as practical jokers.

At about 8:00 p.m., Frank Mahon walked into the office of Attorney John P. Kirk and asked him to accept a retainer as counsel in a criminal case as

Max Brother's Saloon was on the southwest corner of Michigan Avenue and Washington Street. This 1893 photograph shows how the building looked in 1913. The building still appears very much the same today. *Used with permission of the Ypsilanti Historical Society.*

he, Frank, had just killed a man. Kirk suspected that a joke was being played on him but was not sure until Tom Mahon and Edward Kennedy entered the room. Kirk accepted an invitation to join them for a few minutes, while Tom and Frank Mahon and Edward Kennedy called on friends. At about 11:00 p.m., the men ended up on the corner of Washington and Congress, now Michigan Avenue, by the Max Brother's saloon.

At this time, Edward Kennedy conceived the idea of a joke on Frank Mahon, and he called Ypsilanti police officer August Rehil aside and pointed to Frank Mahon. "There is a bad man," said Kennedy. "He is planning to pick the pockets of those men; you better take care of him."

Officer Rehil, who was new to the department, went to Frank Mahon and began to question him, asking his name, the purpose of his visit and other information. Frank Mahon became indignant at being questioned. He grabbed hold of Rehil, and a struggle followed.

Kennedy entered a cigar store where Tom Mahon was lingering. "Your brother Frank is in trouble," said Kennedy to Tom, "and you had better go out and see about it."

Tom left the store and crossed the street to where Frank and Rehil were standing. Tom Mahon was a tall, well-built man with the appearance of a

Hewitt Hall stood on the northeast corner of Michigan and Washington Streets and may have been where Tom Mahon was shot. *Used with permission of the Ypsilanti Historical Society.*

splendid physique. He also had a blustering manner, which may not have helped the situation. What was not apparent was that Tom Mahon was handicapped, as he was missing his lower limbs. He had lost his legs while a student at the University of Michigan Law School: he was traveling to visit his family in Detroit when he fell under a train. Mahon had learned to walk on artificial limbs. This was not obvious from his walk, as Mahon walked with a slight limp and the use of a cane. Officer Rehil may have felt intimidated by the sudden appearance of Tom on the scene.

Rehil ordered the two men to stop and throw up their hands, adding, "I mean what I say."

Frank fell back as Tom continued toward Rehil. Some witnesses would later say that Tom raised his cane. Rehil later said that Tom made a motion as if reaching for a gun. At this, Rehil pulled out his revolver and fired. The bullet struck Tom in the left side. The bullet entered above and to the outside of his heart, penetrated his left lung and lodged in his back. Tom staggered back into the cigar store and cried, "My God, boys, I'm shot."

Kennedy and the others were still in a jolly mood and thought Mahon was joking.

"Quit your kidding," said Kennedy.

"Yes I am," insisted Tom, pulling open his coat and exposing his bloodstained waistcoat. "Call a priest."

Then they noticed how pale his face was and knew that he was clearly in distress. Mahon was placed on a billiard table, and Doctors Post and George Hull treated him as best they could and stopped the bleeding.

As the doctors worked on Tom, Kennedy asked who did it.

"The officer did it," answered Tom, "He was fifteen or twenty feet from me when he pulled a revolver from his pocket and shot me. He had no excuse to shoot me." Then Tom added, "Get a priest here just as quick as you can." Kennedy asked Tom if he was in fear of his life, and Tom said that he was, adding that he had made a will.

Rehil now entered the poolroom and insisted that Tom Mahon be searched for a weapon. The crowd in the room turned hostile toward Rehil, who backed down, so no search was carried out. It was never determined if Tom Mahon carried a weapon. The doctors said he had to go to the hospital in Ann Arbor at once.

Tom Mahon, who was Catholic, again asked for a priest. As soon as the wound was dressed to stop the bleeding, he was taken to Ann Arbor by automobile. On the way, they stopped at the home of Father Frank Kennedy, the pastor of St. John the Baptist Church on Cross Street. Father Kennedy came out to the car. Mahon declared that Rehil had no cause to shoot him.

"Prosecuting Attorney George Burke is making an investigation of the affair and will see the wounded man as soon as the attending physicians permit it," noted the *Ann Arbor Daily Times* of Monday, October 13, 1913. "However, it is thought that Rehil, who is a new man on the Ypsilanti police force, acted as any other man would have under the circumstances, and that Mahon was the unfortunate victim of another of those practical jokes which so frequently lead to harm and which, for all that, are not tabooed by those who ought to know better."

Tom Mahon recovered from his wound and resumed his practice of law in Detroit.

Officer Rehil remained with the Ypsilanti Police Force until 1917, when he left to join the city fire department. That same year, his second wife began divorce proceedings against him. Rehil left the city soon after.

Death on the Huron

The early pioneers of Washtenaw County were drawn to the area in part because of the flowing waters of the Huron River. One aspect of the river the pioneers liked was the fall of the water in several places, making these sites good for mills. The fall of the water would power the works from which came grain, wheat or paper. In time, the mills were powered by electricity, and then, as time passed, most of the mills were replaced with electric power plants. This is what happened at Geddes, a settlement between Ann Arbor and Ypsilanti.

The paper mill that had stood at Geddes was replaced early in the twentieth century with a power station. Such stations, as with all machinery, need maintenance from time to time. For this reason, employees of the Detroit Edison Company went to the station at Geddes on Sunday, August 6, 1916. Two of these men gave their names as William Pritchard and Edward McGill. When the work of the day was done by early afternoon, Pritchard and McGill procured a canoe and several bottles of beer and set off on what was most likely intended as a restful, quiet afternoon.

At about 8:30 p.m., F.C. Stanford, Roy H. Curtis—both of Detroit—and James Williamson, of Ypsilanti, found the body of Pritchard floating in the river. At first it was believed that Pritchard and McGill had fallen out of the canoe they had been riding in and drowned. The body of McGill, however, as well as the canoe, was nowhere in sight.

A couple spends a peaceful time on the Huron River. Prichard and McGill had planned to spend the day in such a manner but left death and a mystery instead. *Used with permission of the Bentley Historical Library, University of Michigan.*

The body was hauled ashore and the authorities notified. A deep wound was found on the side of Pritchard's head when pulled from the river. Washtenaw County coroner Samuel W. Burchfield came and took possession of the body, which was taken to the Moore undertaking rooms at Ypsilanti.

The men who had pulled the body of Pritchard from the river told authorities that they had seen Pritchard and McGill earlier in the day. The two had apparently been drinking and were intoxicated. Authorities learned that Pritchard and McGill had stopped to borrow matches from a party of African Americans from Detroit who were camping by the river. Pritchard and McGill quarreled among themselves while with the group. They also flirted with the female campers and were seen blowing kisses to the women as they set off. The campers heard a splash soon after the pair had departed from the campsite. It was assumed that Pritchard and McGill had fallen from the canoe and drowned at that time.

An autopsy upon the body of Pritchard was carried out the next morning by Dr. A.S. Warthin of the University of Michigan. After the autopsy, Dr.

Warthin declared that the blow to Pritchard's head was sufficient to have killed him instantly, and he had been dead some time before being thrown into the river. The blow could have been struck by an oar, a paddle or some other blunt instrument. Further strengthening the theory of murder was the fact that there was no water in Pritchard's lungs. Suspicion of murder fell on McGill, who was still missing on Monday.

"Strengthening the theory that McGill is only missing because he slipped to shore, and away from the vicinity, is the fact that officers found the canoe in which the men were riding, drawn up on the opposite side of the river from where Pritchard's body was recovered," reported the *Ann Arbor Daily Times News* of Monday, August 7, 1916. There were those who doubted that McGill could have killed Pritchard, as Pritchard was physically the larger of the two and McGill was a hunchback.

On the afternoon of Tuesday, August 8, 1916, deputies pulled the body of McGill from the bottom of the river near where the body of Pritchard had been recovered two days before. The condition of the body was described as terrible after so long in the water. The fact that the body of McGill had been found on the bottom of the river would indicate that his lungs were filled with water and he had most likely drowned. The body was also said to have been covered with cuts and severe bruises, which would indicate that McGill had been attacked. This may have been only the first impression on finding the body. The body was in such a state of decomposition that no attempt at a postmortem was made. "There was no way of determining from the body of McGill, the extent of any injuries which he might have sustained, save a few scratches about the mouth," reported the *Ann Arbor Daily Times News* of Wednesday, August 9, 1916.

"With fellow workmen who were acquainted with both McGill and Pritchard swearing that both were quiet, inoffensive men and that neither was drunk as was first reported, officers are turning their attention to other clues that are developing," noted the *Daily Ypsilanti Press* of Tuesday, August 8, 1916.

The inquest into the case was held in the offices of Justice Thomas in Ann Arbor on Monday, August 14, 1916. The first witness at the inquest was J. Carver, an employee of the Edison Company. He said he had seen Pritchard and McGill the morning of the day they died, and that neither was in a quarrelsome frame of mind. Further, said Carver, he was sure the two had not known each other until that morning when they were introduced. On

Prichard and McGill boarded at the Murdock house at 319 North Huron Street on the southwest corner with Cross Street. The house was demolished in 1935 to make room for a gas station. *Used with permission of the Ypsilanti Historical Society.*

this Carver may have been mistaken, as Pritchard and McGill were said to have boarded at the same house in Ypsilanti. Carver also said both men had considerable sums of money on their persons. He knew this, as Pritchard had cashed a check for seventeen dollars, paid five dollars to one man and should have had ten or twelve dollars on his person. McGill, said Carver, had a ten-dollar bill in his possession on the morning of the day he died. No account of the case states whether the money was found on the bodies.

"McGill, or as Carver called him, 'Shorty' was a good canoeist. He did not know whether McGill or Pritchard could swim," reported the *Daily Ypsilanti Press* on Tuesday, August 15, 1916. Carver did say that McGill had requested a couple of bottles of beer from him.

"All those who gave testimony claimed that when they saw the men they were orderly. The coroner stated that Pritchard probably had drunk some beer and McGill about six bottles," noted the account.

After the inquest, Chief Cain and Deputy Sheriff John Connors said they firmly believed, as they had from the first, that Edward McGill and William Pritchard had known each other before arriving at Ypsilanti and had an old grudge. As the two were paddling along the river, the grudge was renewed, resulting in a quarrel. Pritchard, they believed, struck McGill in the mouth. Then McGill hit Pritchard in the head, over the left eye, with his paddle. The force of this blow was sufficient to cause Pritchard to die instantly, causing his body fall into the river. The body falling into the river caused the canoe to overturn, and McGill, who most likely could not swim, drowned.

This was the theory, but there was little evidence to support it. The theory fit all the known facts, but in the end, it was no better than an educated guess.

"Coroner Burchfield," reported the *Ypsilanti Record* of Thursday, August 17, 1916, "stated he does not have any hopes that the mystery will ever be cleared up."

The only remaining business in the case was to inform the families of Pritchard and McGill of their deaths. This was more difficult than expected, as the families of the two could not be found. Pritchard had said he was from Boston, and McGill had said he was from Cairo, Illinois. Authorities in each city were sent full descriptions of the men in the hope of finding their relatives. In each city, these investigations failed to find the families of the two. Deputy Connors noted that it was unlikely that either man had given his real name, and this was the reason for the failure to find their families or anything about their backgrounds.

In the end, all that was left was a mystery.

Blood on the Schoolhouse Floor

When Irma Casler awoke on the morning of Thursday, March 27, 1919, she had reason to feel mixed emotions about the coming day. On the one hand, the day before she had received a letter from the man she loved, Arthur Baldwin, who was serving with the army in France. On the other hand, she was receiving unwanted attention from another man, Robert Warner, who was persistent and troublesome in his actions. Although she had cause to feel concern, she had reason to be grateful for the path her life had taken. Irma could not have known this was going to be the last day of her life.

At the age of nineteen, Irma was a teacher at the Rentschler district school near Saline. This was her first year of teaching at the school, and she was popular with her students, their families and the community. For Irma, this was a place where she had found happiness. Happiness was not something she had always known. Her mother had died not long after her birth in a railroad accident. After the accident, she was cared for by the family of Mr. and Mrs. Clarence Casler of Aurelius, Michigan, who became so attached to the girl that they accepted her as a daughter of their own, although they never went through the formality of a legal adoption. Irma had even stopped using her birth name of Perkins and went by the name Casler. She attended school in Saginaw for one year and two years at Plymouth, Michigan, where she was the art editor of a school publication. For this she received high

Irma Casler. Detroit News, *Saturday, March 29, 1919.*

honors at her graduation. She was a teacher at Plymouth for a year and then moved on to the Rentschler School near Saline.

Somehow in her short life, Casler had come to know and fall in love with Arthur Baldwin, of Port Huron, who was employed as a fireman on the Grand Trunk Railroad. This was the time of the First World War, and Arthur Baldwin became a private in the army. Baldwin wanted to marry Casler but was concerned about the future. He was aware of the possibility of death and of disabling wounds. Arthur told Irma he could be maimed for life and she had better not wait for him. A few days before he sailed for France, Irma sent him a photograph of herself. On the back of the picture she had written: "Have faith in me and I will be true to you no matter what happens." This photograph would become Arthur's most cherished possession.

At first the two exchanged letters, and then the letters from Baldwin stopped. For several months, Irma waited for some word from Arthur and began to fear he was dead. Finally, a letter arrived written by an army nurse at a hospital in France. The letter informed Irma that Arthur was alive but had been wounded in a gas attack. The attack had left Arthur blind, but the doctors hoped he would recover sight in one eye. Later, because of the treatment he received at the hospital, Baldwin wrote to tell Irma he would recover his sight in both eyes. "I am coming back a whole man," Baldwin wrote, "and then I want to take care of you all the rest of your life."

In another letter, Baldwin wrote:

I am trying to sleep in my tent, but the rumble of a truck train prevents. It is loaded with the boys who are going home, and they are singing the songs we used to sing. I am glad there is no more "No man's Land" and the boys can sing once again the old songs with a real meaning. "Don't Cry Little Girl, Don't Cry," is the one they are singing now, and I can picture you in your little dark skirt and firm little brown boots and pink waist. That's a combination of American girlhood, sweet and neat, and in remembering you, so—I love you.

Arthur Baldwin. Detroit News, *Saturday, March 29, 1919.*

In another letter, Arthur wrote to Irma: "Your letters have done so much to hold me up to manhood. Temptations are many in the Army, but I remembered the little girl back in Mason and passed temptation by. I wanted to be so I could go again to church beside you on a summer's evening with the bells ringing and singing in the twilight."

Baldwin wrote in another letter: "But my eyes are better now. I'm coming home to take care of you, little girl. I have been taught many things over here and most of all, how much I love you.

"Good night, sweetheart," Baldwin concluded. "I am going to sleep now and dream of you and our happiness to come." This was the last letter Irma would receive from Arthur.

Irma added each letter Arthur wrote to a thick packet containing some fifty letters. There were letters, photographs and postcards from other men with the army in France, but the ones from Arthur predominate. Clearly, as far as Irma was concerned, he was the one for her.

Irma may not have been in a good mood on the morning of March 27, 1919, as there was cause for concern. The cause for concern was Robert Warner, who had become something of a problem. Irma had visited friends in Jackson, Michigan, a few months before and had renewed the acquaintanceship with Robert, whom she had known as a child. Until this visit, the two had not seen each other in years. Warner was born in Jackson, Michigan, on April 9, 1902. Robert lied about his age and enlisted in the army in 1918, a few months before the war ended. He received an honorable discharge from the army in February 1919 while at Camp Custer.

To end the unwanted attention of Warner, Irma wrote to him to say she was going to marry another. She told Warner he must stop paying her attention at once. In response, Warner wrote back to say he was coming to see her. "Keep Tuesday and Wednesday for me!" he wrote. "Make no dates on those days, for I am coming to see you." Irma threw the letter in the stove the minute she read it. Then she called Warner and told him not to see her again. After she made the call, those who were close to Irma thought she seemed uneasy and fearful that Warner might come. The following Monday, Irma received a letter from Warner to inform her that he would arrive on either Tuesday or Wednesday.

Warner arrived at the house of Jacob Luckhardt, with whose family Irma boarded, on Wednesday evening. He had visited Irma at the house and stayed there three or four times before. The two quarreled, and Irma refused to have anything to do with him. Warner argued, pleaded and threatened Irma. Finally, Irma refused to answer him at all. Jacob Luckhardt decided to do something to be rid of Warner so he would stop pressing his attention on Irma. In the morning, Warner refused to pay for his lodging. Jacob and his wife thought they now had a chance to make it so unpleasant for Warner that he would never come again. For this reason, Jacob called Deputy Sheriff Cook in Saline and asked Cook to arrest Warner for evading his board bill.

Before Cook could arrive, Irma set out for the schoolhouse, after reading the most recent letter she had received from Arthur Baldwin. Warner asked if he could walk with her to the schoolhouse. Irma emphatically told him no and would not allow him to walk with her. Neighbors along the road saw Irma walking alone, with Warner walking behind and on the opposite side of the road. Behind them came Clara Luckhardt, the sixteen-year-old daughter of Jacob and his wife. Clara stopped at the schoolhouse gate for a few minutes. Then she saw the door to the schoolhouse burst open and Warner rush out.

When Clara entered the schoolhouse, she found that desks had been torn loose and books scattered about. Her teacher, Irma, lay unconscious in a pool of blood, bleeding from wounds in her right breast, her right shoulder, her throat and two wounds in her head. Clara ran to the house of the nearest family, where she told a Mr. Fred Niebling what she had found. He hurried to the schoolhouse, where by this time Irma had regained consciousness. She was now seated on one of the rear benches with her head bowed over a desk. Blood was flowing from the wounds in her head. Niebling thought Irma was bleeding to death. He asked her if Robert Warner was the man who had shot her. Irma said nothing but nodded her head.

On the floor where she had laid were later found four bullets and four empty cartridge shells almost in the pool of blood. Two of the bullets were misshapen and flattened, and one had had a tiny piece of flash hanging onto its ragged edges. Warner may have attacked Irma as she was trying to build a fire in the schoolhouse stove. The doors to the stove were open, and the coal bucket and other fire utensils were scattered about the room.

The county sheriff was notified, and a doctor was summoned. Because of the condition of the roads, the doctor arrived at the schoolhouse an hour after he was called. After a brief examination, the doctor determined that Irma had to be taken to the University Hospital in Ann Arbor. The doctor, with the assistance of George Renz, a member of the school board, helped

Irma to the doctor's car. As the three walked, Irma asked them to careful of her arm, as it was very painful. The doctor drove Irma to the hospital as fast as conditions of the roads would allow.

The *Ann Arbor Daily Times News* of Friday, March 28, 1919, reported:

> *According to the report of the physician in whose care she had been, the bullet that lodged in her right lung would have killed her, had no other bullet been fired. But there were other bullets. One entered her head from the nose, indicating that Warner had shot her when her head was thrown back in a struggle to get away from him. The bullet that entered her head through the nose penetrated the brain, and in some manner became split, after being fired, passing through the skull in two different places. The wound in the head caused three blood clots to form in the brain, and in an effort to remove these clots, and by a possible miracle save the girl's life, surgeons operated yesterday afternoon. She rallied after the operation, but her strength was too far spent to save her, even had there been no bullet in her right lung. The wound in her shoulder would not have caused her death.*

At the hospital, Washtenaw County prosecuting attorney Jacob Fahner was able to ask a few questions of Irma, but only a few, because of her condition. To each question, she gasped out an answer. When asked who shot her, Irma gasped, "Warner."

At 9:00 p.m. that night, Irma regained consciousness sufficiently to gasp: "Arthur, I waited—good bye." Then she died.

As Irma was dying in the University of Michigan Hospital, Robert Warner was sitting nonchalantly in the county jail one mile away. That morning, when Sheriff Peck received the call informing him of the shooting, he sent Deputy Sheriff J.W. Robison and Deputy Sheriff John Connors to investigate. Peck then called Deputy Sheriff Cook at Saline. Cook arrived at the schoolhouse at the same time as the doctor. After a brief examination, Cook met Robison and Connors on the road, and the three set off after Warner.

The trail of Warner led them to the southwest, to the village of Manchester. Many people had seen Warner as he made his way. Cook arrested Warner as he was walking into the village on the railroad track. When arrested, Warner said nothing and was carrying a .38-caliber revolver. Every chamber of the gun was loaded, and there was evidence of the weapon having been recently fired. He made no effort to resist arrest when taken into custody. Warner was taken to the county jail at Ann Arbor, where he arrived a little before 1:00 p.m. When questioned at the jail, Warner maintained a smiling, nonchalant attitude. To those questioning him, he said, "Oh yes, I shot her. What time is it?" When asked why he had killed Irma, Warner answered, "I can't tell," or said, "I won't tell." He never gave a motive for his crime.

"He is a good-looking, well set up fellow, a bit above the average height. He strikes me as a keen fellow and bright," said Sheriff Peck to the *Ann Arbor Times News* on Friday, March 28, 1919. "How such a man could have brought himself to commit such a crime I cannot understand."

Immediately after being informed of the death of Irma, Washtenaw County coroner Samuel Burchfield impaneled a jury and held the first formal session of the inquest over the body in the undertaking rooms of F.R. Muehlig. The jury was composed of Charles Dawson, Frank Painter, Robert Schumacher, William Eldert, Fred Moehn and Lee Thomas. The jury was then adjourned, to be called back if needed. The body of Irma was then turned over to her foster family, who had it moved to the village of Aurelius, where the funeral was held and the body buried in the local cemetery.

Warner stood at attention like a soldier before his commanding officer on the morning of Friday, March 28, 1919, as the warrant charging him with murder was read. He was dressed in the uniform of the United States Army, with a silver stripe on the left sleeve, indicative of six months' service. Above the stripe was a silver star, denoting volunteer enlistment. He stood before the justice without his leggings and with his shoes muddied. Still, he had something of a debonair appearance. Occasionally during the proceedings, something of a smile drifted across his face. When the warrant was read, Justice Thomas asked Warner if he wanted legal advice. Warner instantly replied that he did not.

"Do you understand that this case is try-able only before the circuit court and that you may either demand an examination here or waive examination?" Justice Thomas asked.

Warner answered, "I do."

"What do you care to do in this matter?"

"I waive examination," responded Warner.

Warner was remanded to the county jail, without bail, to await trial.

"I have no regrets," said Warner, perhaps in an interview with reporters, "no sorrow. I am glad I did it. I would do it again, exactly as I did it Wednesday, and under the same circumstances. I was justified."

Warner denied that he was in love with Irma and said he had no wish to marry her.

"I had not seen her for 10 years, until less than three weeks ago," he said. "She started the trouble by asking me to write to her."

"Were you jealous of this chap in France?"

"I don't even know his name," he answered. "I don't know where she met him or anything about him. What is his name?"

"Then this theory that you were madly in love with the girl is wrong?"

He laughed faintly. "I had not seen her since I was a kid. She came to visit my mother. I have seen her only a few times and that within this month."

"I went to the Luckhardt house because I wanted to know something and to get something," Warner explained. "I found out what I wanted to, I got what I wanted, and then I killed her, just as I had thought maybe I might do if I should find out what I did, and just as I would do again, if time were to turn back a week."

"And what was it that you found out that made you want to kill that little girl?"

"That I can't say," he answered.

"Weren't you sorry when you saw her lying in a pool of her own blood?"

"No," he said, smiling with mirthless lips, "I am not sorry. I have never been sorry, and I never expect to regret what I did Thursday, morning."

The court had appointed George Burke as attorney for Warner. On Saturday, March 29, 1919, Burke petitioned Judge Leland for a sanity commission to examine Warner and determine if he was sane. The court appointed three physicians—Dr. H.H. Cummings, Dr. Theophile Klingmann and Dr. John Wessinger—to inquire into the state of Warner's sanity. The doctors met with Warner for two hours on Saturday afternoon and for three hours on Sunday afternoon. Warner's father was present for the meeting on Sunday. The three doctors filed their findings with the court on Monday, March 31, 1919:

> *Honorable Judge Sample:*
> *Dear Sir: As directed, I have on two occasions examined Robert Warner as to his sanity. In my opinion Robert Warner is insane and suffering from that form of insanity known as the paranoid type of dementia precox [sic]. My opinion is based on the following history and facts:*
> *1. In his early school days Robert Warner would suddenly absent himself from school, without giving any explanation. At one time he was out of*

school for nearly three months. His parents noticed during the last seven years times when their son seemed lost in thought, and was not easily aroused from these times of apparent deep thought.

2. *Examination shows a young man in good health physically. He is lucid and oriented as to time and place. His memory is good. There is a constant defiant attitude at all times and a frequent grimace and silly expression. His left eyelids are forced into a squint frequently.*

3. *He admits premeditated plan to kill his school teacher friend in case he found out certain things, and gives as these things her statements, that she would show his letters and force him to support her.*

4. *He is satisfied that his action was the only solution of his problem to protect her friends and his relatives from disgrace. Under the same circumstances he would do it again.*

5. *He has a second motive for killing that he has not disclosed to his lawyers or to anyone. This he refuses to state, although he feels that it would clear him and justify his action before the court and the whole world. This idea is so fixed that it is my opinion that is a delusion.*

6. *He is absolutely without emotion.*

7. *No physical changes take place while he tells of the killing of his friend. His expression at this time is one of satisfaction.*

The prognosis in the form of insanity is bad. I believe it will progress until there is marked mental deterioration.

[Signed] *H.H. Cummings*

At the same time, Dr. Theophine Klingmann independently submitted his findings as well. He found that Warner was insane and suffering from a progressive form of insanity known as paranoid dementia praecox. He based his findings on the following:

1. *A marked immutability of a fundamental fixed idea, apparently a delusion with reference to some great moral wrong which was aimed to destroy him and his family.*

2. *Absolute faith in his delusion.*

3. *Marked premptness [sic] and intensity of his actions is shown in his procedure in committing the crime and no regret for his action.*

4. *Absolute justification in his own mind of committing the crime and no regret for his action.*

The State Hospital for the Criminally Insane at Ionia, where Robert Warner was expected to spend the rest of his life. *From* Michigan Manual, *1913.*

5. Absolute loss of affectivity even under the most trying circumstances.
6. Characteristic defiant and suspicious attitude.

Dr. Wessinger noted that Warner was afflicted with progressive paranoia that had begun several years before and was accompanied with delusions both persecutory and homicidal. He noted this condition would increase in severity. He added: "Such persons being dangerous to society if at large; I advise that he be placed under rigid restraint for an indefinite time."

Dementia praecox is a term no longer in use. Today, Warner would most likely have been diagnosed as having a form of schizophrenia.

Warner had told the doctors he was sorry for one thing: not that he had killed Irma, but that the shots had not entered a vital organ so her life would have ended without suffering. He said he was sorry to see her lie there on the floor suffering but was glad he had shot her and was glad she was dead.

Robert Warner was taken before Judge Sample on Tuesday, April 1, 1919, and, on the recommendation of Prosecuting Attorney Jacob Fahrner, was committed to the state hospital for the criminally insane at Ionia. This was after testimony of Doctors Cummings, Klingmann and Wessinger concerning his mental state and after they said that his stories about the murder were the product of a disordered mind. Other witnesses included Sheriff Pack, Clara Luckhardt and Jacob Luckhardt. The examination was only a formality so that there would be a court record of the case to form the basis for his commitment to the asylum.

Arthur Baldwin, the man for whom Irma waited, returned to the United States by early June 1919. Broken in health and spirit, he arrived in New York to learn the details of the case for the first time. He had only an inkling of the case from a brief account in the Paris edition of an American newspaper. When still in France, Baldwin had been moved from one hospital to another so often that he had only received one letter after the murder. "Only a few weeks before she died," said Baldwin, "she wrote me and said she was lonesome and wished I would come back. I replied, trying to cheer her, and urged her to go out and meet lots of people and enjoy life."

"At the time I was fearful of losing my eyesight," continued Baldwin, "and I wrote her that I would not expect her to wait for a blind soldier. I never received any reply, although I presumed she wrote one, but her attitude toward the man who killed her was answer enough. She was true blue."

Baldwin said he did not know what he would do. He was in class 3-B, which meant he was not in good physical shape and still needed care. His eyes were still weak, and he expected to be sent to the hospital at Camp Custer or to a hospital in Detroit. He said he would like to go to Cuba or someplace far away from the man who broke his heart.

When Robert Warner was sent to the state hospital for the criminally insane at Ionia, it was expected that he would remain there for the rest of his life. Warner died at the age of seventy-five on May 19, 1977, in San Francisco, California.

Irene the "Bandit Queen"

At midnight on Monday, January 4, 1926, two men armed with sawed-off shotguns entered the ticket office of the Michigan Central Railroad Depot in Ypsilanti, at the corner of Cross and River Streets. The armed men forced A.F. Esslinger to lie down on the floor and ordered W.T. Truax to open the safe and cash drawer. The armed men took $15.85 of New York Central Railroad money, $153.25 of Michigan Central money and $100.00 in Pullman funds. Then the men tore the telephone off the wall. As they were leaving, one of the men left a parting message: "Tell Chief Connors, Shorty is back." To make their escape, the men fled to a waiting taxicab parked on East Cross Street, less than a block from the depot.

What Ypsilanti chief of police John Connors made of the message is not known, but he was aware of a series of robberies of gas stations and other businesses that had occurred beginning just before Christmas in Ypsilanti, Ann Arbor, Saline and Milan. Police in Hamtramck had arrested Edward Masciski, who owned the car used in the robbery at Ypsilanti and of a jewelry store in Hamtramck.

The car had been abandoned by the robbers as police closed in. In the car were found penny wrappers from an Ann Arbor bank that had been held up. Masciski answered the description of one of the robbers. He said

The Michigan Central Railroad Depot in Ypsilanti at Cross and River Streets, as it appeared when the Kozak Gang held it up. *Used with permission of the Ypsilanti Historical Society.*

the car was stolen and had reported it as stolen to the Hamtramck police the week before. Detroit and Hamtramck officers had a number of suspects in custody, but witnesses were unable to identify any of them as having taken part in the crimes. Masciski was released.

"Meanwhile," reported the *Daily Ypsilanti Press* of Friday, January 8, 1926, "local officers and Michigan Central detectives are following each clue which develops. Thursday night a local taxi company took two men to Hamtramck who insisted on being driven by the Warren Avenue route rather than Michigan Avenue. Their conversation en route was all regarding robberies but nothing has developed to indicate they were not in Ypsilanti on legitimate business."

The account told of a car answering the description of the car used in the Michigan Central robbery stopped at a Ypsilanti garage with three men in it. The men called for gasoline, but instead of answering the call, the owner, Ted Schaible, went out the back door to call police. By the time the police arrived, the car had driven off.

When the victims of the robberies were unable to identify the suspects then held in custody, police showed them photographs of men suspected of an attempted bank robbery at Cassopolis in November. All of the witnesses were able to identify Philip Kozak, Frank Doing and Jimmie Nelson as the robbers. The three had criminal records. Now the police had clues to follow.

The police had other clues as well. These included a midnight call by a young woman from a little store in Ypsilanti for a taxi to take three men to Hamtramck. The caller said the men would be waiting on South Huron Street.

There was also a clue from a Detroit police officer who had overheard a conversation in a Detroit gambling house involving a young woman whose mother had married a rich Ypsilanti farmer who had sold his property to the Ford Motor Company and moved to a place near Britton.

Somehow on Saturday, January 16, police learned that the robbers were staying at the farm of John Barlow near Ridgeway. That evening, Adrian police officers led a force of ten men, including Chief John Connors and Washtenaw County undersheriff Dick Elliott, to the Barlow farm. Officers arrived at the farm and surrounded the house only to learn that they had missed the men by five minutes. Detectives were left at the house to prevent any communication with the men. Some of the other officers left the farm to go to the DeRousie garage in Ridgeway to arrest Stuart DeRousie, as he was believed to have driven the men from Hamtramck to the farm, Ypsilanti and other places. It was not then known if DeRousie was a member of the gang (known as the Kozak Gang) or only a driver.

Connors and the other officer were informed that Philip Kozak was expected back at the Barlow farm Sunday night and two other members of the gang would be in Detroit. Kozak returned to the farm as expected and was traced by police to the barn, which was surrounded. Police found Kozak, also known as "Shorty," unarmed and asleep in the hay. "He was just a yellow cur when we cornered him," said Chief Connors later. "He has confessed the local robberies and the Detroit jobs." Kozak was wanted by police at this time as a suspect in the murder of a Detroit police officer and the wounding of a Detroit police detective.

When police searched the barn, they found several sawed-off shotguns, homemade ammunition, in which lead and steel were used for shot, and a number of revolvers. Among the items found in the barn were gold chains and diamonds stolen from a jewelry store in Hamtramck.

The *Daily Ypsilanti Press* of Monday, January 18, 1926, reported:

> *Barlow, when questioned by police, admitted he knew the men who been about the place were Detroit criminals. At first they had carefully guarded their identity, but lately they have been open in discussing their activities and*

informed Barlow if anyone came to the place for them they intended to shoot to kill. He told Chief Connors he had not dared tell anyone who they were, or their business, and that he had been too closely watched to send any word to friends in or about Ypsilanti, of his present predicament.

A second arrest at the Barlow farm was that of Mrs. Barlow, who was charged with aiding and abetting members of the gang at the farm. When arrested, Mrs. Barlow was wearing jewelry stolen from a store in Hamtramck. She was accompanied to the jail by her five-year-old grandson Earl, the child of her daughter Irene. Mrs. Barlow had lived most of her life in Ypsilanti and had been married to a man named Walling, who had died. She had married John Barlow on June 20 of the previous year. The story she told police did not match the one told by her husband. She said the men came to the farm asking for room and board. One, she claimed, said he worked for Ford, and the other was employed in a Detroit garage but had been laid off or was sick, so she took them in.

The *Daily Ypsilanti Press* of January 19, 1926, wondered:

Just why should Mrs. John Barlow dressed in her neat blue serge, with just a bit of blue silk slip showing beneath, with her fine silk hose and good shoes, have to be taking in boarders, boarders sick, and out of jobs? How does it happen that she was wearing jewels believed to be part of the loot taken in a Hamtramck jewelry store robbery? Didn't she know her boarders had filled the barn with sawed off shot guns, revolvers and ammunition?

What else may be true of Mrs. Barlow. There is no gainsaying that she is neat and orderly. The bed and cot in the detention room are straightened and neat. She has placed the old rug on the floor for her little grand son to play on, washed out his little cover-alls in the tiny wash basin, spread clean newspapers on the bench. The scratched, marred walls, scribbled on by other visitors with less respect for city property, annoy her. She would like to clean them.

When Mrs. Barlow expressed concern that the experience would leave its mark on Earl's memory, Chief Connors offered to take the child to the home of her sister, who lived in the city. She turned this down, explaining that she could not bear to let him go.

Visitors to the jail brought Earl some toys and a new pair of coveralls. Mrs. Barlow ordered a new pair of shoes for the child. When a visitor arrived at the jail, Mrs. Barlow would instruct the child to tell them who the first four presidents of the United States were. The child would then do as told.

"The first four presidents of the United States were Washington, Adams, Jefferson, Madison."

"Lansing is the capital of Michigan."

"Columbus discovered American in 1492."

"My name is Earl Smith. I was born in 1920. My father lives in Chicago. He's a singer."

"And he was an Elk and a Mason, wasn't he?" prompted his grandmother. Earl nodded his head.

To the merchant who dropped off the new pair of shoes for Earl, she said, "I'm sorry to have to meet you this way. Have them charged to John Barlow. He can afford to pay for them." Then she instructed Earl to tell the man who the first four presidents of the United States were.

That same day, Mrs. Barlow was released and told not to leave the city. Police in Detroit arrested her daughter Irene Walling Smith that same afternoon.

When police searched the Barlow home, they found a letter with information about which train Irene and Frank Doing, another member of the gang, were expected to arrive at Detroit on. Chief Connors was with Detroit police when Irene arrived at Detroit, as he was the only one who knew Irene by sight. Officers expected Irene and Frank to come together, but Irene came alone.

"She was keen looking all right when she got off that train," officers told the *Daily Ypsilanti Press* for a story that was published on Monday, January 25, 1926. "Salmon colored coat, trimmed with fur, dark hat, henna hair, and make-up that was a work of art."

Irene Walling Smith would become known as the "Bandit Queen" of the Kozak Gang.

The *Daily Ypsilanti Press* of January 26, 1926, noted:

> Irene, the bandit queen, queen of Shorty Kozak's gang of killers and robbers, is not unknown in Ypsilanti. Her mother has lived here nearly all her life, Irene went to school here when she was a little girl, grew up here, worked here. They know her down Rawsonville way, where her grandmother, Mrs. Henry Leonard lives. She played with the youngsters in the little village when she was a child.

"Yes," said her grandmother, Mrs. Leonard, to the *Press*, "I know Irene's in trouble: I guess she has her mother in trouble too. Young folks today are too careless of the company they keep. I'm sorry for them both, but I'm too old to try to help them now. When you get around 80 you can't do much."

"Yes, Irene was wild, all right," recalled Chief Connors. "We had complaints about her and her mother too, when they lived up on Summit Street for awhile two or three years ago, and we threatened to raid the place if they didn't move, so they left."

"Little Earl," continued Connors, "Irene's five year old son was just a baby then and he didn't know anything about the presidents he so glibly prattles about now."

"Irene was wild all right," said Connors, "but I didn't suspect her then of becoming a bandit queen."

Her stepfather, John Barlow, called her a bandit queen. "Christmas Eve," he told police, "after the oil station robberies in Ann Arbor, the boys came in and dumped the money all on the kitchen table here. Irene counted it out among them: 'This for you, Jimmie, this for you Frankie, this for you Shorty, and this for me.' Her mother sat in that chair there, and I sat here."

Barlow was asked why he never told anyone about the gang:

> *I didn't dare. One day I said some thing to one of the neighbors about not liking the boarders we had at our house and Irene heard of it. She came in that night and says to me, "John, you've been squawking. You know what happens to squawkers, don't you?" And right then our barn was loaded with sawed-off shotguns and revolvers. I've hardly dare to eat.*
>
> *Queen of the mob? You'd think so if you heard them quarrel over her. They went to Montreal after the first robberies in Ypsilanti, Irene and Jimmie and Frankie, to Frank's mother's house. Frank told me how his mother put her arms around Irene and says, "Frank, why don't you marry this sweet little girl and settle down?" Then Jimmie got jealous, and after they got back to Detroit Frank got suspicious he was going to bump him off, so after the Michigan Central job in Ypsilanti Frank went back to Montreal to stay. He told me he was going to get a job there and quit the gang.*

Irene had nothing to say to police when arrested. In her purse they found an address for Frank in Montreal. Police in Montreal arrested Frank that same day, and he was soon after returned to Detroit. This left

Irene Walling Smith, the "Bandit Queen" of the Kozak Gang. Daily Ypsilanti Press, *Monday, January 25, 1926.*

only one member of the gang still at large: Jimmie Carson, who was also known as Nelson.

"They'll never get Jimmie," said Irene. "He's the only one of the gang I loved. And they'll never get him, not alive, at least."

By now, police had come to the conclusion that Jimmie Carson was the brains and leader of the Kozak Gang and was the most dangerous of them all. Now Philip Kozak was saying it was Carson who had killed a Detroit police officer named Rusinko and wounded a Detroit detective named Mickley. Mickley had recognized Kozak while in a Hamtramck restaurant and tried to arrest him. Kozak admitted that he had been at the scene of each shooting but claimed it was Carson who fired the shoots.

At this time, police arrested Clarence Airietta, the man who had driven the cab for the robbers on the night of the Michigan Central robbery. For his driving, the robbers had given him a fifty-dollar tip. Charges were later dropped, as he had not taken part in the robbery and had informed his employers of the fare to Ypsilanti.

On Friday, January 29, Nettie Barlow, who was now confined in the Lenawee County jail with her daughter Irene on charges of aiding and abetting criminals, was served with a copy of a bill of divorce filed that day by her husband, John. Representing John was his second cousin, Leon D. Barlow, who was the son of Walter Barlow, who was then chief assistant corporation council of the city of Detroit. The Barlow family had long been residents of Rawsonville, and both Walter and Leon were well known in the small community. Another longtime family at Rawsonville was the Jacksons, including Nettie and Irene. Nettie's mother, Mrs. Leonard, still lived in Rawsonville in a modest home near the little white church.

"While the divorce bill charges Mrs. Barlow with 'disregarding the solemnity of her marriage vow' and being 'guilty of extreme cruelty' it outlined more specifically her association with members of the Kozak gang as the grounds upon which Mr. Barlow seeks divorce," reported the *Daily Ypsilanti Press* of Saturday, January 30, 1926.

John Barlow stated in the bill that it was on about December 6 that Irene first introduced the gang to him. His wife, he charged, "appeared to know the gang and was on intimate terms with them." The bill of particulars contained the charge that Nettie made trips to Detroit with members of the gang and loaned her car to the gang.

The members of the gang would no longer have need of a car, as Philip Kozak was sentenced to fifteen years imprisonment and Frank Doing was sentenced to thirty years on Wednesday, February 3, 1926. The judge ordered both sent to the prison at Marquette. The two admitted to twenty holdups in the Detroit area and pleaded guilty. They were not tried for crimes committed in Washtenaw County but would have been if convictions had not been secured in Detroit. At that time, Jimmie Carson was the only member of the gang still loose. Carson was arrested soon after by Detroit police because of a tip provided by Irene. He was arrested on the evening of Sunday, February 6, when he was lured into a trap set by police when he thought he was going to meet Irene.

"A natural blonde, he had dyed his hair black and was wearing a mustache when arrested,—a disguise which had enabled him to brush shoulders with detectives on his trail the past few days he has admitted," reported the *Daily Ypsilanti Press* of Tuesday, February 9, 1926.

Irene told police she would have stuck with Jimmie if he had not started killing people. She said she had no use for a killer. Jimmie claimed that she turned against him because Frank Doing had captured her affections.

After Jimmie was arrested on Sunday night, the warrant charging him with murder was issued Wednesday morning. At the examination, Carson pleaded guilty to homicide in the first degree. In a few months, Carson had netted $20,000, but that morning he did not have the money to retain a lawyer. After conferring with a court-appointed attorney, he reiterated the plea of guilty. Carson claimed he was not the one who had killed Rusinko but decided, he said, with so much evidence against him that he "might as well plead guilty and get it over with." The next day, just after noon on Thursday, February 11, 1926, the judge sentenced Carson to life imprisonment. The twenty-seven-year-old Carson claimed the sentence of life meant nothing to him as a bullet was, he said, working its way to his heart and would kill him in two or three years anyway.

"The only thing I regret is the money I spent on Irene," said Carson to the *Daily Ypsilanti Press* of Friday, February 12, 1926. "Why, I've spent $200, $300 in one night and most of it showing her a good time. And then she turns me up, huh? So that's the kind of an oil can she is!"

On Wednesday afternoon, Nettie Barlow filed her answer to the charges made by her husband John in his bill of divorce. She denied "disregarding the solemnity of her marriage vow" or being a "woman of low moral habits who associates with criminals." She said the first time she saw the gang was ten days before Christmas, when they came with Irene. Nettie said it was some time before she knew they were something other than the auto workers they claimed to be.

"The bill sets forth they asked [John] Barlow if he would like a drink and he expressed his willingness to take a drink whereupon Doing and Carson provided the plaintiff with moonshine whiskey from which he drank liberally and became very friendly…and told them they might stay as long as they liked and it was agreed they should pay $10 a week board and room." She further stated that the property where the gang was found belonged to John and not to her and the gang had remained at his invitation. Additional charges of "indecent, vile, dirty, filthy habits" and "stingy, miserly, penurious" financial habits were made against John.

No longer the "Bandit Queen," Irene and her mother Nettie returned to the village of Rawsonville and lived near her grandmother, Mrs. Leonard, where she found work and supported herself and her son Earl. Irene cared for her mother during her last illness, and Nettie died in February 1929. Then Irene found work in a Trenton boardinghouse. There, she and Earl contracted typhoid. In the early morning hours of Monday, August 26, 1929, Irene died at the age of twenty-seven. Irene was buried in a little cemetery near New Boston in a grave beside her mother. Earl was expected to recover, and his father in Chicago was informed of Irene's death. The father, the *Press* noted, might come for the now nine-year-old boy or he might not. Should the father fail to come, Earl would be cared for by his great-grandparents, the Leonard family. "The Leonard's," noted the *Ypsilanti Daily Press* of Wednesday, August 28, 1929, "are loyal to their own."

Bibliography

Beakes, Samuel W. *Past and Present of Washtenaw County.* Chicago: S.J. Clark Publishing Co., 1906.

Chapman, Charles C. *History of Washtenaw County, Michigan.* Chicago: Charles C. Chapman & Co., 1881.

Colburn, Harvey C. *The Story of Ypsilanti.* N.p.: 1923.

Doll, Louis Wm. *Less than Immortal: The Rise and Fall of Frank Porter Glazier of Chelsea, Michigan.* N.p.: 1992.

Peckham, Howard H. *The Making of the University of Michigan 1817–1967.* University of Michigan Press, 1967.

Reasoner, James M. *Michigan Reports: Cases Decided in the Supreme Court of Michigan from December 10, 1909 to February 3, 1910.* Vol. 159.

DEATH OF PATRICK DUNN

Michigan State Journal. "Trial of Charles Chorr for the Murder of Patrick Dunn," December 29, 1843.

BODY SNATCHING AND THE UNIVERSITY OF MICHIGAN

Ann Arbor Courier. "Body Snatching," Friday, June 21, 1878.

———. "Body Snatching Again," Friday, July 5, 1878.

————, Friday, April 12, 1878.

————, Friday, June 14, 1878.

————. "Medical Science, Dissector," Friday, August 9, 1878.

————. "More Body Snatching," Friday, July 12, 1878.

Ann Arbor Register. "A Body-Snatching Case," Wednesday, April 10, 1878.

————. "A Mistake," Wednesday, July 3, 1878.

————. "Too Late," Wednesday, July 10, 1878.

Huelke, Donald F. "Troubled Times for the University—Body Snatching in Michigan." *Washtenaw Impressions*, October 1962.

Kaufman, Martin, and Leslie L. Hanawalt. "Body Snatching in the Midwest." *Michigan History* (Spring 1971).

New York Times. "The Cincinnati Body-Snatchers," Sunday, June 2, 1878.

————. "Death of John Scott Harrison," Wednesday, May 29, 1878.

————. "The Graveyard Robbers," Friday, May 31, 1878.

————. "The Ohio Grave Robbers," Wednesday, June 19, 1878.

Waite, Frederick C. "Grave Robbing in New England." *Bulletin of the Medical Library Association* 33 (July 1945).

The Rapalje Riot

Ann Arbor Courier. "Ann Arbor Savings Bank," Friday, November 8, 1878.

————. "The Riot," Friday, November 8, 1878.

————. "Supposed Suicide," Friday, November 1, 1878.

Ann Arbor Register. "Suicide and Riot," Wednesday, November 6, 1878.

Detroit Free Press. "Disgraceful Riot," Friday, November 1, 1878.

————. "Suicide," Thursday, October 31, 1878.

Evening News. "College Rumpus," Friday, November 1, 1878.

Michigan Argus. "A Disgraceful Affair," Friday, November 1, 1878.

Burning the Normal Organ

Evening Times. "The Escape Was Narrow," Monday, November 13, 1899.

————. "Has Aroused the Council," Tuesday, November 14, 1899.

Normal College News, November 21, 1899.

Superintendent of Public Instruction for the State of Michigan for the Year 1878. N.p.: W.S. George & Co., 1879.

Ypsilanti Commercial. "It Might Have Been," Thursday, November 16, 1899.

———. "A Musical Event," Friday, April 2, 1886.

———. "State Normal School," Saturday, August 10, 1878.

———. "Tried to Burn the Normal," Thursday, January 4, 1900.

THE MYSTERIOUS DEATH OF WILLIAM BENZ

Ann Arbor Courier-Register. "Coroner's Inquest Says It's Murder," Wednesday, September 2, 1903.

———. "A Foul Murder Was Committed," Wednesday, August 26, 1903.

Daily Argus. "It Is Still a Deep Mystery," Tuesday, August 25, 1903.

———. "Says It Is Possible but Not Probable," Thursday, August 27, 1903.

———. "William Benz Found with His Throat Cut," Saturday, August 22, 1903.

Detroit Free Press. "It Was Murder," Friday, August 28, 1903.

Detroit News. "Jury Says It Was Murder," Friday, August 28, 1903.

———. "Murder Mystery in Washtenaw," Saturday, August 22, 1903.

Evening Times. "The Body Is Still Unburied," Thursday, September 1, 1903.

———, Wednesday, September 2, 1903.

Washtenaw Daily Times. "Another Circumstance Against Suicide Theory," Wednesday, August 26, 1903.

———. "Coroner's Inquest Says It's Murder," Thursday, August 27, 1903.

———. "Details of Benz Inquest," Friday, August 28, 1903.

———. "It Looks More Like Murder Than Ever," Monday, August 24, 1903.

SCIO NIGHT RAIDERS

Ann Arbor Daily News. "Boys Gave Bail," Wednesday, July 15, 1908.

———. "Echoes Are Heard," Saturday, July 18, 1908.

———. "Nasty Pranks," Tuesday, July 14, 1908.

Ann Arbor News-Argus. "Auto on Fire," Wednesday, November 13, 1907.

Detroit Free Press. "Nine Farmers Fined for Raids on Stock," Wednesday, July 15, 1908.

Detroit News. "Eleven Young Farmers in July as Night Raiders," Tuesday, July 14, 1908.

Ypsilanti Daily Press. "Accuse Men of Burning Auto," Thursday, July 14, 1908.

———. "Scio Feud Has Lasted 20 Years Monday," July 20, 1908.

———. "Young Farmers Night Raiders," Wednesday, July 15, 1908.

LODI TOWNSHIP SHOOTING

Daily Times News. "Mother Saw Her Son Kill Himself," Monday, May 3, 1909.

Ypsilanti Daily Press. "Lodi Township Youth Accidentally Kills Self with Revolver Sheriff and Police Scout Attack Story," Monday, May 3, 1909.

BODY IN THE BARN

Ann Arbor Daily Times News. "Aged Chelsea Woman Murdered and Slayer Gets Away Safe," Friday, September 26, 1913.

————. "If Stapish Death Is Case of Suicide It Is Queerest on Record," Saturday, September 27, 1913.

————. "Mystery Is Yet Unsolved," Monday, September 29, 1913.

Chelsea Standard. "Was It Murder?" Thursday, October 2, 1913.

Detroit Free Press. "Find Aged Chelsea Woman Murdered in Barn Back of Home," Friday, September 26, 1913.

————. "Scouts Idea that Woman Is Suicide," Saturday, September 27, 1913.

Detroit News. "Little Old Lady of Lurid Garments Dies Mysteriously," Friday, September 26, 1913.

SHOOTING OF ATTORNEY MAHON

Ann Arbor Daily Times. "Another Joke Ends Wrong," Monday, October 13, 1909.

Daily Ypsilanti Press "Detroit Attorney Is Shot by Officer Rehil; Result of Joke," Monday, October 13, 1913.

Detroit Free Press. "Attorney T.J. Mahon Shot as He Menaces Ypsilanti Policeman," Monday, October 13, 1913.

————. "Strife in Ypsilanti Over Police Affairs Back of Mahon Case," Tuesday, October 14, 1913.

DEATH ON THE HURON

Ann Arbor Daily Times News. "Autopsy Shows Man Was Killed by Heavy Blow," Monday, August 7, 1916.

————. "Body of McGill Found in River This Afternoon," Thursday, August 8, 1916.

————. "Tragedy of the Huron River Is Still Mystery," Wednesday, August 9, 1916.

Daily Ypsilanti Press. "Believe McGill Killed Pritchard," Tuesday, August 15, 1916.

————. "Edison Employee Killed in Drunken Fight Sunday," Monday, August 7, 1916.

————. "Inquest Next Monday," Friday, August 11, 1916.

————. "McGill Body Found, Bruised Like Pritchard," Tuesday, August 8, 1916.

Ypsilanti Record. "Huron Tragedy Still Unsolved," Thursday, August 17, 1916.

————. "Murder Is the Theory," Thursday, August 10, 1916.

Blood on the Schoolhouse Floor

Ann Arbor Daily Times News. "Jackson Soldier Shoots Teacher in Love Quarrel," Thursday, March 27, 1919.

————. "Pretty Victim of Robert Warner Dies of Wounds," n.d.

————. "Robert Warner Has No Regrets He Says Today," Saturday, March 29, 1919.

————. "Warner Goes to Ionia for His Crime," Tuesday, April 1, 1919.

————. "Warner Insane Is the Finding of Physicians," Monday, March 31, 1919.

Daily Ypsilanti Press. "Lover of Slain Girl Is Home from France," Thursday, June 5, 1919.

————. "Slain Teacher Dead, Youth Held for Fatal Shots," Friday, March 28, 1919.

Detroit Free Press. "Soldier-Lover Kills Teacher," Friday, March 28, 1919.

Detroit News. "Death Hallows Oversea Troth," Friday, March 28, 1919.

————. "Glad He Killed Teacher," Saturday, March 29, 1919.

Ypsilanti Record. "A.A. Baldwin Has Returned," Thursday, June 5, 1919.

————. "Ionia for Boy Killer," Thursday, April 3, 1919.

————. "Lodi Teacher Shot Six times by Young Lover," Thursday, March 27, 1919.

Irene the "Bandit Queen"

Daily Ypsilanti Press. "Bandit Queen's Tip Aids Police, Slayer Caught," Tuesday, February 9, 1926.

———. "Bandits' Acquaintance Basis for Divorce Suit," Saturday, January 30, 1926.

———. "Cab Driver for Robbers Caught," Friday, January 29, 1926.

———. "Career of Ypsilanti Girl as 'Bandit Queen' Involves Family, Leads Gang to Police Trap," Monday, January 25, 1926.

———. "Detroit Bandit Gang Leader Under Arrest," Monday, January 18, 1926.

———. "Jimmie Carson, Bandit Leader, Sentenced to Life Imprisonment," Thursday, February 11, 1926.

———. "Jimmie Carson a Gunman Since a Lad of Thirteen," Friday, February 12, 1926.

———. "Little Lad Companion of Grandmother in Jail," Tuesday, January 19, 1926.

———. "'Shorty's Gang' Returns to Rob Ticket Offices," Tuesday, January 5, 1926.

———. "Suspected Thug Not Identified," Wednesday, January 6, 1926.

———. "Third Member of Detroit Gang in Custody," Tuesday, January 19, 1926.

———. "Two Members of Kozak Gang Given Terms in Prison," Thursday, February 4, 1926.

———. "Typhoid Claims Last of Once Notorious Kozaks," Wednesday, August 28, 1929.

———. "Victims Unable to Identify Any of Ten Suspects," Friday, January 8, 1926.

About the Author

James Mann is a local historian, storyteller and author in Ypsilanti. His books include *Ypsilanti: A History in Pictures*, *Ypsilanti in the 20th Century*, *City of Ypsilanti Fire Department 100 Years*, *Footnotes in History* and *Our Heritage: Down by the Depot in Ypsilanti*, written with Tom Dodd. He has been a local history columnist for over ten years.

Visit us at

www.historypress.net